Language *for* Learning in the Secondary School

Language for Learning in the Secondary School employs the same easy-to-use format as the best-selling primary version of this book but has been adapted to meet the specific needs of secondary school teachers. This indispensable resource is packed full of practical suggestions on how to support students with speech, language and communication difficulties.

Colour-coded throughout for easy referencing, this unique book supports inclusive practice by helping teachers to:

- identify students with speech, language and communication needs (SLCN);
- understand how language is processed;
- consider roles and responsibilities at secondary level;
- plan a differentiated curriculum;
- consider the language demands across the subjects;
- adopt a whole-school approach;
- make use of a wide range of positive strategies;
- empower students to access the curriculum.

Language for Learning in the Secondary School comes complete with a wealth of photocopiable resources and activities, giving teachers and teaching assistants the confidence to help students with speech, language and communication needs more effectively in mainstream settings. It will also be an extremely useful resource for specialist teachers, speech and language therapists and educational psychologists.

Sue Hayden is a speech, language and communication needs trainer with over 30 years' specialist teaching experience both in primary and secondary schools.

Emma Jordan is a specialist speech and language therapist for the Speech & Language Therapy Service within Worcestershire NHS Children's Services.

Both authors provide training for practitioners working with children and young people of all ages with SLCN and manage the 'Language for Learning' project based in Worcestershire.

nasen is a professional membership association which supports all those who work with or care for children and young people with special and additional educational needs. Members include teachers, teaching assistants, support workers, other educationalists, students and parents.

nasen supports its members through policy documents, journals, its magazine *Special!*, publications, professional development courses, regional networks and newsletters. Its website contains more current information such as responses to government consultations. **nasen**'s published documents are held in very high regard both in the United Kingdom and internationally.

Language *for* Learning in the Secondary School

A practical guide for supporting students with speech, language and communication needs

Sue Hayden and Emma Jordan

Routledge
Taylor & Francis Group

LONDON AND NEW YORK

nasen
Helping Everyone Achieve

First published 2012
by Routledge
2 Park Square, Milton Park, Abingdon, Oxon OX14 4RN

Simultaneously published in the USA and Canada
by Routledge
711 Third Avenue, New York, NY 10017

Routledge is an imprint of the Taylor & Francis Group, an informa business

British Library Cataloguing in Publication Data
A catalogue record for this book is available from the British Library

Library of Congress Cataloging in Publication Data
Hayden, Sue.
  Language for learning in the secondary school: a practical guide for supporting students with speech, language and communication needs/Sue Hayden and Emma Jordan.
  p. cm.
  Includes bibliographical references and index.
  1. Language arts (Secondary) 2. English language–Composition and exercises–Study and teaching (Secondary) 3. Literature–Study and teaching (Secondary) I. Jordan, Emma. II. Title.
  LB1631.H338 2012
  428.0071′2–dc22
                                                                            2011010375

ISBN: 978-0-415-61975-2 (pbk)
ISBN: 978-0-203-81844-2 (ebk)

Typeset in Goudy
by Wearset Ltd, Boldon, Tyne and Wear

Contents

Acknowledgements

We would like to thank NASEN for the opportunity to develop a practical resource book for secondary schools, and in particular Lorraine Peterson and Beverley Walters for their support and encouragement.

Thanks also go to the many practitioners nationwide who have given us positive feedback following use of the original *Language for Learning* book. We have been asked many times for a secondary version and hope this book will provide the support practitioners need at Key Stages 3 and 4.

As always, many thanks go to the Language for Learning team of trainers for sharing their ideas, supporting us in our development work and inspiring us in their commitment towards supporting children and young people with speech, language and communication needs.

Speech, Language and Communication Framework (SLCF)

> The SLCF is a clear and detailed framework of the skills and knowledge in speech, language and communication which are important for everyone who works with children and young people.
>
> (The Communication Trust 2008)

The SLCF is available as an interactive online tool for practitioners to use to evaluate their own knowledge and skills. The tool provides links to training and resources to support on-going professional development. The SLCF defines competencies at four stages: universal, enhanced, specialist and extension. The stages range from the knowledge and skills that everyone working with children and young people should have – i.e. universal through to advanced and specialist learning around speech, language and communication needs.

Making practical use of *Language for Learning in the Secondary School* will help practitioners to develop knowledge and skills in the following areas of the SLCF:

Strand A: Typical speech, language and communication development and use	
Universal	A1/2/4/5/6/7/8/9
Enhanced	A3/4/5/6
Strand B: Identifying and assessing SLCN	
Universal	B1/2/3/4/5/6
Enhanced	B1/2/3/4/6/7
Strand C: Positive practice	
Universal	C1/2/3/4
Enhanced	C1/2/3/4/5/6/8/9/10/11/12/13/14/15/16/17

Strand D: Speech, language and communication and behaviour, and emotional and social development	
Universal	D1/2
Enhanced	D1/3/4/5
Strand E: Roles and responsibilities and how services are structured	
Universal	E1/2/4
Enhanced	E1/2/3/4
Strand F: Special educational needs in educational settings	
Universal	F1
Strand G: Parents, carers, families, peers and friends	
Universal	G1
Enhanced	G1/2/3
Strand H: The effects of professional development in speech, language and communication	
Universal	H1

Introduction

The original *Language for Learning* book was first published in 2004, winning the NASEN and *Times Educational Supplement* (*TES*) Book Award for Teaching and Learning in 2005. The book has proved to be highly popular with practitioners as it offers an easy-to-use format, is quickly accessible and packed with practical ideas to support primary-aged children experiencing speech, language and communication needs (SLCN). Sue Hayden and Emma Jordan have worked in partnership for over ten years within the wider Language for Learning project, developing practical training and resources to support practitioners working in mainstream settings. This self-funding, not-for-profit project is jointly owned by Worcestershire County Council and Worcestershire PCT, supporting a joint, collaborative approach towards meeting SLCN.

As highlighted by the recent Bercow Review (DCSF 2008), the demands and challenges continue as children with SLCN move from primary to secondary school. However, there is minimal evidence of on-going support or services at secondary age. In response to the Bercow Review, there has been an increase in availability of supporting literature for secondary schools, produced by The Communication Trust. This has been supported by a developing evidence base (Joffe 2011; Wilson *et al.* 2010; Stringer 2006).

This book has been developed to provide a practical guide for secondary school practitioners, utilising the same easy-to-use format as *Language for Learning*.

It aims to help readers to:

- understand speech, language and communication skills;
- increase their awareness of SLCN at secondary age;
- recognise and identify students experiencing SLCN;
- understand the link between language and behaviour, social and emotional development;
- understand the roles and responsibilities of secondary staff;
- consider the language and communication demands within the secondary curriculum;
- make use of a wide range of positive strategies to support access to the curriculum and social opportunities.

Key to Symbols

Areas of Speech, Language and Communication

Within Chapter 2, areas of speech, language and communication are identified and described. For ease of reference, these areas are both colour- and symbol-coded throughout the book.

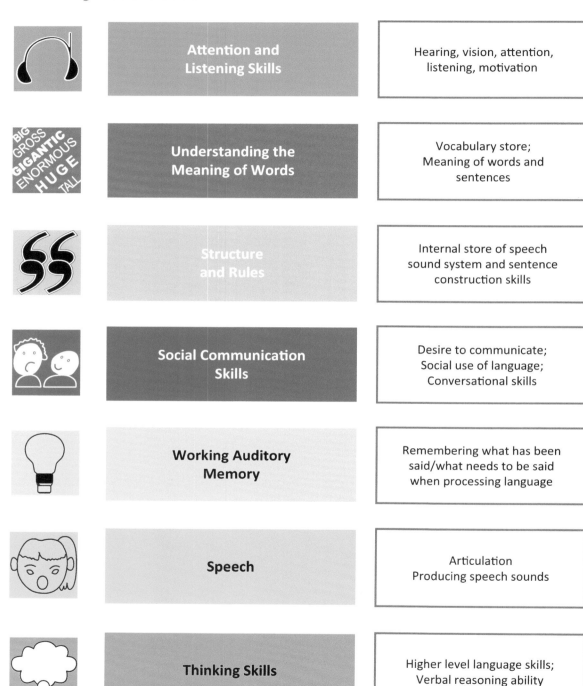

	Attention and Listening Skills	Hearing, vision, attention, listening, motivation
	Understanding the Meaning of Words	Vocabulary store; Meaning of words and sentences
	Structure and Rules	Internal store of speech sound system and sentence construction skills
	Social Communication Skills	Desire to communicate; Social use of language; Conversational skills
	Working Auditory Memory	Remembering what has been said/what needs to be said when processing language
	Speech	Articulation Producing speech sounds
	Thinking Skills	Higher level language skills; Verbal reasoning ability

Levels of Support

This book provides an extensive range of strategies and approaches to support practitioners in meeting the needs of young people with SLCN. To intervene in a systematic way, it is necessary to consider different levels of support. The concept of a tiered system at a universal, targeted and specialist level provides a framework for supporting young people (DfES 2003). Throughout the book, the level at which strategies and approaches can be used will be identified:

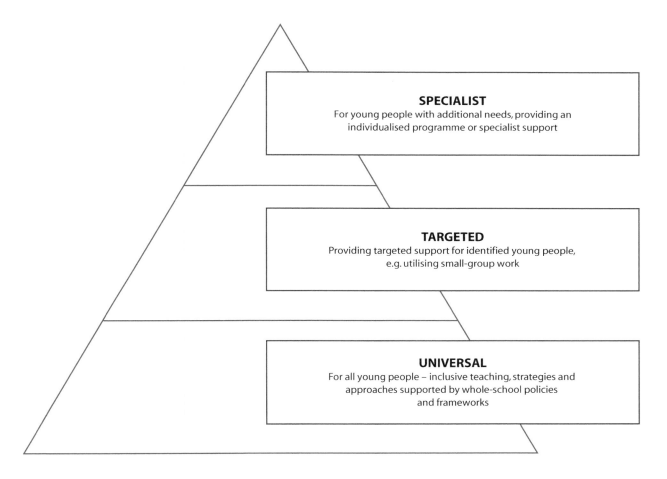

SPECIALIST
For young people with additional needs, providing an individualised programme or specialist support

TARGETED
Providing targeted support for identified young people, e.g. utilising small-group work

UNIVERSAL
For all young people – inclusive teaching, strategies and approaches supported by whole-school policies and frameworks

Making Practical Use of this Book

The structure of the book can be seen below to allow readers ease of access, whether considering how to meet the individual needs of a student or planning a whole-school approach.

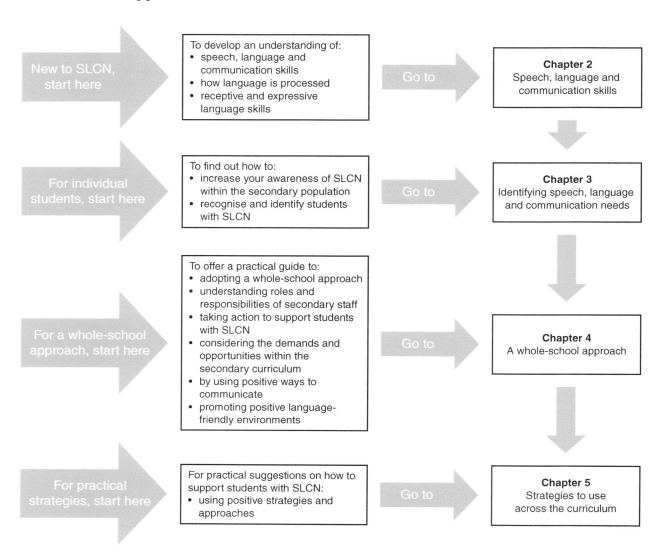

Speech, Language and Communication Skills

This chapter aims to provide practitioners with an understanding of speech, language and communication skills and a shared language to talk about language. It describes the theoretical Language for Learning model of speech, language and communication skills; identifies and defines areas of speech, language and communication; describes how language is processed; and explains the difference between receptive and expressive language skills.

The Language for Learning Model of Speech, Language and Communication Skills

The process of understanding and using language is a complicated one, involving a range of different skills. The Language for Learning model provides a structured approach – a framework for thinking and talking about speech, language and communication skills. The model provides a shared language to talk about language skills; this prevents confusion and can help break down communication barriers created by the use of terminology, particularly by outside agencies. Often, teaching staff simply do not know where to begin to support a student with SLCN. The model can be used to make sense of observations and assessments, pinpointing specific needs and strengths. As specific areas of language are identified, it is possible to identify areas for development and intervention with confidence. Each area of language is colour- and symbol-coded, allowing all subsequent chapters to give reference to the model.

The Language for Learning model of speech, language and communication skills can be seen here.

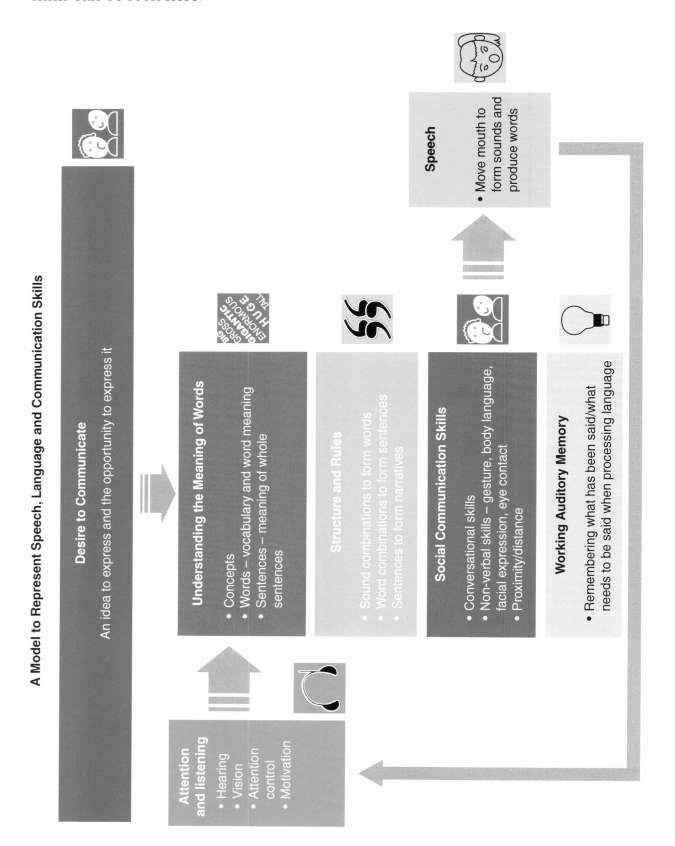

A Model to Represent Speech, Language and Communication Skills

Desire to Communicate
An idea to express and the opportunity to express it

Understanding the Meaning of Words
- Concepts
- Words – vocabulary and word meaning
- Sentences – meaning of whole sentences

Structure and Rules
- Sound combinations to form words
- Word combinations to form sentences
- Sentences to form narratives

Social Communication Skills
- Conversational skills
- Non-verbal skills – gesture, body language, facial expression, eye contact
- Proximity/distance

Working Auditory Memory
- Remembering what has been said/what needs to be said when processing language

Speech
- Move mouth to form sounds and produce words

Attention and listening
- Hearing
- Vision
- Attention control
- Motivation

The boxes on the model represent different skills:

Desire to Communicate

This is a fundamental communication skill – the desire to communicate an idea to someone else for either social reasons or to meet a personal need. Young people need an idea to communicate, the desire to communicate this idea to another person and the opportunity to do so. This skill is part of 'social communication skills', as described below.

Attention and Listening

This encompasses a range of skills: the ability to hear what has been said; to attend and listen to those involved in the conversation, both the speaker and others listening; and being able to sustain this attention for the relevant length of time. It also involves motivation, being interested in what the speaker has to say. In addition to auditory information, young people need to be able to attend to the visual information provided – i.e. the non-verbal communication skills being used, together with any relevant contextual information. It is also necessary to identify and then eliminate any redundant information, such as extraneous noise or other distractions.

Understanding the Meaning of Words

This is the ability to understand and use vocabulary – words, concepts and sentences. It is a vocabulary store supported by our semantic memory skills. The meaning of the word is stored (e.g. for a concrete object such as a 'Bunsen burner'), along with what we use it for, where we might find one, the parts it has, the group of words it belongs with and what it looks like. The semantic system is structured and highly organised, with words stored by association with other words. Vocabulary development continues through secondary school, with young people adding to their understanding of vocabulary through exposure within practical, real-life experiences and through reading. Knowledge of word meanings is developed over time through repeated exposure across a range of experiences. All new vocabulary introduced within the curriculum relies on this system working effectively.

Structure and Rules

This relates to the set of rules that govern our language system. Literacy development is highly dependent upon these skills. There are three key skills in this area:

- Phonology: the rules that govern how sounds are combined to form words; our speech sound system. In addition to storing the meaning of the word, we also store the sound sequence, so we know that 'car' is made up of two sounds – 'c' and the long vowel 'ar'. Phonological awareness, developed within the Foundation stage, is the ability to think consciously about these sounds and to use these skills within literacy (Speake 2003). One would expect a young person to have both semantic and phonological knowledge of a word – i.e. understand its meaning and its sounds structure (e.g. number of syllables).

- Syntax: the rules governing word order, the way in which we combine words to form sentences and sentences to form longer narratives.

- Morphology: the changes made to the beginnings and endings of words to indicate a change in meaning; e.g. adding an 's' to indicate a plural so 'car' becomes 'cars'.

Social Communication Skills

The ability to understand and use language in social situations. Skills in this area include conversational skills such as maintaining a topic of conversation, waiting for a turn to speak and non-verbal communication skills such as understanding and use of eye contact, facial expression, proximity and touch. These skills are essential for the development of emotional understanding, social relationships and appropriate social behaviour. Young people continue to develop social communication skills through secondary school, developing greater sophistication in the use of language for both social and academic reasons.

Working Auditory Memory

This is the ability to remember information for a sufficient period of time in order to process it and to understand its meaning. It also provides speakers with feedback, keeping track of what has been said and what still needs to be said. Working auditory memory *capacity* is determined by the end of Key Stage 1, with any future development focusing on strategies to support it.

Speech

This is the ability to co-ordinate the mouth to produce the sounds to make words.

We generally associate language development with early years. However, language and communication skills continue to develop throughout the secondary phase. Students continue to learn new vocabulary, develop use of complex language structures and become more sophisticated in their use of social language (The Communication Trust 2010a).

Receptive and Expressive Language

There are two ways of entering the model:

Receptive Language Route

In order to understand language (i.e. receptive language) the following route is taken:

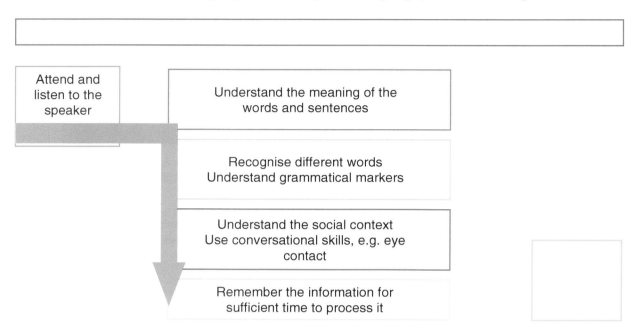

Receptive language involves all of the language areas. In order to process information and instructions, all areas of language are active and in use.

Expressive Language Route

In order to use language (i.e. expressive language) the following route is taken:

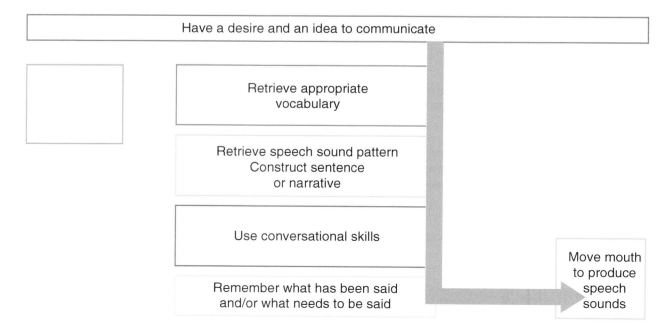

Using language involves many of the language areas. It is worth noting that the term 'expressive language' is often used to refer specifically to the use of vocabulary and sentence construction skills.

 Thinking Skills

Within early years, children develop their abilities to use language for social communicative reasons – i.e. to communicate and interact with others. Language and communication skills are developed and used in real-life, concrete experiences. The demands and opportunities increase as children start school; language is used *for learning* not just for communicating, with the introduction of new vocabulary and social communication rules linked to new social situations and new people. Expectations change as language is used and taught in more abstract and less context-based situations – e.g. talking about objects, events and situations outside of the immediate context. By the secondary phase, 'decontextualised use of language becomes the main medium for teaching and learning' (Ripley and Barrett 2008, p. 8).

Students require higher level language skills to access the secondary curriculum and develop social relationships. They need to demonstrate not only the ability to understand and use language in context, but to use language for thinking – i.e. verbal reasoning. This involves gathering and analysing all of the information available: the language used; the social situation; any hidden intent or implied meaning; and others' viewpoints. These skills are required for students to develop their ability to make inferences, predict what will happen next, give explanations and express ideas, thoughts and feelings. To succeed in secondary school, students require these higher level language skills, enabling them to use language 'for negotiation, compromise, to resolve conflict, develop relationships and for managing and regulating their emotions' (The Communication Trust 2010a, p. 6).

Identifying Speech, Language and Communication Needs

This chapter aims to increase understanding and awareness of SLCN within the secondary population. It provides information about incidence and a description of the different types of SLCN. To help practitioners recognise students with SLCN in the secondary context, key indicators of difficulties are identified within each of the areas of language introduced in Chapter 2. A guide to school-based assessment, including a range of identification tools, is provided. The impact of SLCN on learning and social and emotional development is explored.

Speech, Language and Communication Needs

The ability to communicate is an essential life skill for all young people; it underpins social, emotional and educational development (DCSF 2008). However, there are many students who struggle to develop these skills. The term 'speech, language and communication needs' is used to encompass a wide range of difficulties relating to all aspects of communication (DCSF 2008). It is useful to consider SLCN within three broad sub-groups (Lindsay *et al.* 2010; ICAN 2006):

1 *Primary SLCN*: speech, language or communication difficulties occur in the *absence* of any identified neurodevelopmental or social cause, e.g. a specific language impairment. These difficulties are likely to be both specific and persistent in nature into secondary school.

2 *Secondary SLCN*: speech, language or communication difficulties occur in association with another difficulty, such as a learning, sensory or physical impairment, e.g. SLCN secondary to a hearing impairment or a learning difficulty. These difficulties are likely to be persistent in nature into secondary school.

3 *Transient SLCN*: young people with SLCN associated with limited experiences, typically associated with socioeconomic disadvantage (Lindsay *et al.* 2010). These difficulties are described as *transient*; this suggests that given the right support, children and young people are likely to 'catch up'. However, a significant proportion of young people are reported to continue to

experience receptive and expressive language difficulties within mainstream secondary schools in areas of socioeconomic disadvantage (Myers and Botting 2008; Spencer *et al.* 2006; Spencer 2007).

How Many Young People Experience SLCN?

National prevalence data (ICAN 2006; DCSF 2008; The Communication Trust 2010b) suggests that up to 10 per cent of all children and young people have a long-term persistent communication disability. This includes children with primary and secondary SLCN. This includes:

- about 7 per cent of children and young people experiencing specific and *primary* speech and language impairments;
- 3 per cent of children and young people experiencing SLCN in association with another difficulty (i.e. *secondary* SLCN).

Approximately 50 per cent of children at school entry (reception year) in socioeconomically disadvantaged populations have speech and language skills that are significantly lower than those of other children of the same age. Evidence suggests that these difficulties can be seen in secondary schools. A survey found 75 per cent of students in one inner-city secondary school to have SLCN (cited in The Communication Trust 2010a).

Indicators of SLCN

Students with SLCN often present with a range of difficulties in the secondary environment. The context (e.g. different people and situations) will impact upon a student's skills. Indicators of SLCN within each area of language can be seen below.

 Attention and Listening Skills

A student may be observed to:
- fail to attend to the speaker;
- experience difficulties sustaining attention and listening skills across a variety of contexts;
- lack motivation to listen – those students who are aware that processing auditory information is demanding may 'switch off' or lack motivation to engage in verbal discussions;

Attention and Listening Skills continued

- be more able to engage when visual or kinaesthetic learning opportunities are presented;

- experience difficulties integrating attention, i.e. processing both the auditory and visual information;

- be distracted by redundant information, e.g. extraneous noise;

- experience fatigue following activities that require sustained listening;

- day dream.

 Understanding the Meaning of Words

A student may be observed to:

- have limited or weak vocabulary skills with gaps in everyday vocabulary;

- say 'I've heard that word before', in relation to subject-specific vocabulary, but not be able to demonstrate any understanding of the meaning of a word;

- use or read language without understanding its meaning, i.e. use sophisticated vocabulary but then when questioned be unable to say what the word means;

- experience difficulties learning, retaining and then retrieving subject-based vocabulary;

- learn a word in one situation but then experience difficulties applying it or generalising its use;

- experience difficulties defining words, including identifying similarities or differences between word meanings;

- experience greater difficulty with more abstract concepts, e.g. time concepts such as 'next week', 'last term', 'the day after tomorrow';

- be inflexible with vocabulary, e.g. become confused with words with multiple meanings;

- struggle to find the right word – hesitating, using a similar word, using gesture or mime to compensate or creating new words.

Structure and Rules

A student may be observed to:

- use immature expressive language, such as missing words from sentences or confusing the word order;

- speak telegrammatically, i.e. using only the key words needed to convey a message;

- struggle to understand complex grammatical structures, such as connectives like 'and', 'so', 'but', 'to';

- make grammatical errors in written work;

- struggle to sequence ideas and thoughts, and so have difficulties recalling events in the correct sequence or telling a story in the correct sequence;

- have poor phonological awareness, i.e. sound knowledge of a word;

- experience difficulties learning new words, i.e. storing the sounds for a new word correctly, resulting in inaccurate use.

Social Communication Skills

A student may be observed to:

- lack flexibility in use of language for a range of complex functions, i.e. to compliment others, express feelings, negotiate, suggest or reason;

- experience difficulties with conversational skills, including:
  - waiting for and taking a turn in a conversation
  - initiating and then maintaining a topic of conversation appropriately. A student may have a tendency to talk about a favourite topic
  - repairing a breakdown when there is a misunderstanding
  - awareness of the listener's knowledge, providing either too much or too little information for the listener to understand;

- find it difficult to understand and use non-verbal communication skills, including eye contact, facial expressions, posture and proximity. A student may stand too close to others without realising the implications of this;

Social Communication Skills continued

- speak too loudly for the situation;

- take the adult's role;

- not understand hidden meaning or intent, i.e. making a literal interpretation of what has been said. A lack of use of intent or implied meaning results in a student appearing overly honest or 'blunt';

- struggle to adapt and use language in a flexible way across different social situations.

Working Auditory Memory

A student may be observed to:

- forget instructions easily;

- not record homework accurately (given verbally);

- struggle to follow long and complex instructions despite appearing to listen;

- forget stages within an activity;

- forget equipment;

- respond to just the beginning or the end of an instruction;

- be unable to repeat or recall what needs to be done in the correct order following instruction;

- get lost within an activity or when giving information;

- lose track in a conversation or a discussion. A student may appear to repeat themselves frequently;

- need more time to process language;

- jump to the wrong conclusions or give a tangential reply based on only part of the information given;

- become easily confused, particularly during fast conversations or discussions;

- lack organisational skills.

Speech

A student may be observed to:

- say multi-syllabic or complex words inaccurately;
- simplify words;
- experience difficulties with intelligibility within connected speech;
- be dysfluent, i.e. may stammer.

Thinking Skills

A student may be observed to:

- experience difficulties using language for complex functions, i.e. to reason, evaluate, plan, negotiate, engage in debate;
- struggle to assimilate all of the necessary information leading to misunderstandings;
- fail to consider the viewpoint of others;
- lack organisational skills.

Types of SLCN

As discussed earlier within this chapter, students may experience a primary or secondary SLCN. Potential difficulties within a range of different types of SLCN are presented below to support practitioners in identifying specific needs.

Primary SLCN

Delayed Language Skills (Transient)

In areas of socioeconomic deprivation, students may present with impoverished language or communication skills. Difficulties may present across most/all areas of language.	
Potential difficulties	**Area**
Attention and listening Processing auditory information	
Limited exposure to vocabulary Vocabulary development – breadth and understanding of everyday and subject-specific vocabulary Understanding abstract concepts	
Understanding and use of complex grammatical structures, e.g. connectives, passives Sequencing of ideas to form a narrative	
Understanding social rules Using language appropriately across different situations Conversational skills, e.g. turn-taking Using language for complex functions, e.g. negotiating, evaluating, complimenting others	
Remembering information presented verbally Following lengthy or complex instructions	

Receptive Language Difficulties

'Receptive language' refers to understanding and processing language. At a secondary level, students experiencing receptive language difficulties can be difficult to identify. By this time, students have typically developed reasonable expressive language skills and are using a range of strategies to compensate for poor receptive language, e.g. using visual information, relying on routine, using peers as a source of information and copying their actions.

Potential difficulties	Area
Sustaining attention and listening skills when information is presented verbally or during discussions	
Vocabulary development – breadth and understanding of vocabulary Understanding abstract concepts	
Understanding and use of complex grammatical language Sequencing and organisational skills	
Keeping pace in fast conversations Understanding hidden meaning, non-literal or ambiguous language	
Remembering and recording information presented verbally Following lengthy or complex instructions despite listening Time taken to process language	
Verbal reasoning Organisational skills	

Expressive Language Difficulties

Expressive language difficulties include vocabulary, using language in meaningful sentences and constructing sentences using grammatical knowledge and skills. These difficulties are easier to identify than receptive language difficulties as a student's language may appear immature, disjointed or difficult to follow.

Potential difficulties	Area
Vocabulary development – breadth and understanding of vocabulary Word retrieval skills Ability to use and define both concrete and abstract vocabulary	
Word order Sequencing ideas, forming narratives Use of grammatical knowledge in spoken and written language	
Verbal reasoning Use of language for complex functions, e.g. predicting, explaining	

Specific Language Impairment

A primary and specific persistent receptive or expressive language disorder/impairment, in the absence of any other difficulties. It does not include children or young people who do not develop language because of intellectual or physical disability, hearing loss, emotional problems or environmental deprivation. Identification of SLI will require specialist assessment by a speech and language therapist and specialist teacher/educational psychologist.

Potential difficulties	Area
Vocabulary development – breadth and understanding of vocabulary Defining words Identifying similarities and differences in word meanings Applying or generalising vocabulary Concept development Word retrieval skills	
Word order Sequencing ideas, forming narratives Use of grammatical knowledge in spoken and written language	
Understanding and applying social communication rules Using language effectively in conversations	
Verbal reasoning Use of language for complex functions, e.g. predicting, reasoning, explaining	

Speech Sound Difficulties

With the right support and intervention, speech sound difficulties are likely to have resolved by secondary age. However, there may be students with residual intelligibility difficulties or students experiencing articulation difficulties in association with another difficulty.

Potential difficulties	Area
Phonological awareness skills Speech sound storage for complex multi-syllabic words	
Articulation Intelligibility	

21

Secondary SLCN

SLCN are associated with a wide range of other difficulties. A small range of cognitive, sensory and physical difficulties have been identified below to signpost specific difficulties that may arise.

Learning Difficulties

Students with moderate or severe learning difficulties will experience SLCN across all areas of language.	
Potential difficulties	**Area**
Attention control Listening skills	
Vocabulary development – breadth and understanding of everyday and subject-specific vocabulary Understanding abstract concepts Sorting and classifying skills	
Understanding and use of grammatical structures, e.g. tenses, connectives Sequencing of ideas to form a narrative Phonological awareness skills Rhyming and rhythmic skills	
Using language appropriately across different situations Conversational skills, e.g. turn-taking Using language for complex functions, e.g. negotiating, evaluating, complimenting others	
Remembering information presented verbally Following lengthy or complex instructions	
Verbal reasoning Organisational skills	

Specific Learning Difficulties (SpLD)

Students who have difficulty in acquiring skills in specific areas – literacy, numeracy and organisation – are often articulate and enjoy talking. There can, however, be difficulty with the language of sequencing, auditory discrimination, auditory memory, classifying and organising vocabulary.

Potential difficulties	Area
Sorting and classifying vocabulary Word retrieval skills	
Following instructions that require sequencing skills Auditory discrimination skills Rhyming and rhythmic skills Sound storage for complex multi-syllabic words	
Following lengthy or complex instructions Remembering information given verbally	
Verbal reasoning Organisational skills	

Autistic Spectrum Disorder

Students with an autistic spectrum disorder, e.g. autism or Asperger's Syndrome, experience difficulties with the 'triad of impairments'. The triad covers social interaction, social communication and flexibility of thought. All young people with autism will experience SLCN.

Potential difficulties	Area
Attention control Listening Filtering information, not becoming distracted by redundant information	
Understanding the meaning of words Use of sophisticated vocabulary without understanding Understanding how words are linked by their meaning Defining words Flexibility, e.g. understanding words with multiple meanings Word retrieval skills	
Use of language for social purposes, i.e. beyond personal needs Turn-taking skills Initiating conversations appropriately Maintaining a topic of conversation Use of eye contact Use of appropriate proximity/distance Understanding non-verbal communication, e.g. gesture Understanding and using non-literal or ambiguous language	
Understanding cause and effect in social situations Considering others' viewpoints Using language for complex reasons, e.g. to reason, predict	

Attention Deficit Hyperactivity Disorder

Students experiencing ADHD find it difficult to focus and maintain their attention. They are likely to experience difficulties with cause and effect in social situations; understanding social cues; and maintaining attention and listening skills within lesson time. They experience difficulties applying rules in social situations.

Potential difficulties	Area
Attention control Focusing on the speaker Listening skills	
Understanding how words are linked by meaning Sorting and classifying skills	
Turn-taking skills, waiting for a turn Maintaining a topic of conversation Use of eye contact Recognition of facial expression	
Understanding cause and effect Assimilating information	

Hearing Impairment

The introduction of cochlear implants is changing the needs of this group of young people, but both receptive and expressive language skills may be affected by a hearing impairment.

Potential difficulties	Area
Attention skills Processing auditory information	
Vocabulary development – breadth and understanding of everyday and subject-specific vocabulary Concept development	
Understanding and use of grammatical structures Phonological awareness skills	
Fine-tuning language according to context Understanding social rules Awareness of others Turn-taking skills	
Articulation	

Cerebral Palsy

Students with cerebral palsy may experience associated language and learning difficulties.	
Potential difficulties	**Area**
Attention control Listening skills	
Vocabulary development – breadth and understanding of vocabulary Concept development	
Use of facial expression Use of eye contact Understanding social rules	
Following lengthy or complex instructions	
Articulation	
Verbal reasoning skills	

Developing a Second Language

A child or young person in full-time education does not usually have a problem acquiring a second language, provided that cognitive skills, hearing, speech and social skills are developing typically. Developing a second language to the level where it is possible to *use language for learning* is more challenging and develops over a much longer period of time. A student new to English will require support in developing language skills. If there is a concern about language development, it may be necessary to request an assessment in the student's first language.

Potential difficulties	Area
Attention control Listening skills	
Breadth of vocabulary development	
Understanding and use of English grammatical structures Awareness of the English speech sound system	
Understanding social rules and cultural differences Use of eye contact	
Ability to follow instructions	

Impact of SLCN

Speech, language and communication needs can impact on a student's academic achievement, behaviour, the development of social relationships and emotional development.

Academic Achievement

Children and young people with SLCN are at greater risk of literacy difficulties (ICAN 2006). In turn, these difficulties will impact on a young person's general access to the curriculum and exposure to vocabulary and grammatical understanding, potentially limiting language development further.

Educational outcomes for children and young people with SLCN at School Action Plus and with a statement of special educational needs are considerably lower than for their peers (DCSF 2008):

- Twenty-five per cent of children with SLCN reach the expected levels for their age in English and maths at age 11. Eighty per cent of children achieve the expected level in English – a gap of 55 per cent; the gap in maths is 46 per cent and in science it is 41 per cent.

- At the end of Key Stage 4, 15 per cent of young people with SLCN achieve five GCSE A*–C or equivalent compared to 57 per cent of all young people (National Pupil Database cited in DCSF 2008).

Social, Emotional and Behavioural Difficulties

A significant difference can be seen between primary and secondary school in the number of children with SLCN identified as their primary educational need at School Action Plus. The number of young people identified with SLCN decreases significantly at secondary age, with the number of young people identified as experiencing social, emotional and behavioural difficulties increasing. Longitudinal research tells us that language and communication needs persist beyond the primary stage, calling into question the identification of SLCN at a secondary level (Joffe 2009). SLCN can be misinterpreted as behavioural issues at a secondary age. Students with SLCN can present with the following behaviours:

- a reluctance to engage;

- withdrawing from or avoiding situations that involve interaction with others;

- disruptive behaviour as a result of poor attention and listening skills;

- non-compliance or non-responsive behaviour caused by a lack of understanding;

- time wasting caused by a lack of understanding;

- copying inappropriate behaviour of other students without understanding the consequences;

- difficulty applying social rules and demonstrating appropriate social behaviour;

- signs of anxiety in new situations or at times of change;

- low self-esteem;

- unreliability in giving information verbally, e.g. recalling past events;

- truanting from school.

Young people experiencing SLCN are likely to become increasingly aware of their difficulties during adolescence, leading to increased vulnerability to social, emotional and behavioural difficulties. Forming and maintaining friendships is likely to be challenging for a young person with SLCN, leading to a lack of peer support. As young people with SLCN grow older, they are more likely to have poorer emotional health and there is a stronger likelihood of mental health problems in adulthood (ICAN 2006).

For students with social, emotional and behavioural difficulties, there is significant evidence of unrecognised SLCN. There is also 'evidence that those with undetected communication needs may be at greater risk of exclusion from school' (The Communication Trust 2010a). Research has identified a high incidence of receptive and expressive language difficulties among students at risk of exclusion (Clegg *et al.* 2009).

Research carried out within young offender institutions estimates that 60 per cent of this population have difficulties with speech, language and communication. These difficulties impact upon the young person's ability to communicate effectively with others and prevent them from benefiting from verbally mediated intervention (Bryan 2009, cited in DCSF 2008). This is an area of recent development, with identification tools and resources developed by The Communication Trust, such as the 'Sentence Trouble' resource referred to in Chapter 4.

Identifying SLCN

A joined-up, collaborative approach is essential when identifying SLCN. The necessity for 'early' identification and action *regardless of age* was highlighted by the Bercow Review (DCSF 2008). As discussed above, a student's skills may vary greatly from one situation to another, so it is vital that the team works together to gain a full picture of a student's needs. The majority of young people experiencing SLCN will have been identified before secondary school, so it is essential to consider any historical information available. For some young people, SLCN only become apparent as the demands of the curriculum increase at Key Stage 3; for these students there may not be any evidence of SLCN at an early years or primary level.

It is important to:

1   gather any historical information such as history of SLCN, learning or social needs;

2   observe a student across a range of differing situations;

3   consider speech, language and communication skills, general learning ability, social and emotional development;

4   consider the impact of the environment and teaching situation on a student's skills;

5   seek the student's views;

6   involve parents;

7   gather information from subject teachers;

8   consider the need for further assessment by involving outside agencies.

Observation

Observation is a powerful tool and forms the basis of all of the identification tools within this chapter. Observing a student across a range of contexts can provide a wealth of information about speech, language and communication skills, together with the impact of any needs on social interaction and relationships with others. Observation can also highlight potential issues linked to the environment or teaching style that may impact upon a student's ability to access the curriculum.

Tips for Observation

- Observe the environment and consider your teaching style as well as the student – see Chapter 4 for language-friendly environment tools. This will help you consider the impact of the environment on the student's ability and may change the focus of intervention from the student to the environment and your own communication.

- If you are able, observe the student in situations that *are* and *are not* language-friendly.

- Consider the context and observe in a range of different situations:
  - structured lessons and less-structured times
  - type of activity, e.g. discussion-based, practical lessons
  - teaching situation, e.g. whole class, small group or individual
  - social situations, e.g. transition times, lunch times.

- Think about how you will record the information and observe discreetly:
    - a nudge or prompt sheet with key words to act as a reminder
    - a specific identification tool
    - consider confidentiality and objectivity.

- At secondary age, SLCN can be difficult to spot, so be prepared to become actively involved, asking the student questions to probe further. For example, ask the student to recall information and instructions given verbally; explain their understanding of a lesson; demonstrate understanding of subject vocabulary; or explain homework. You may need to include other students so as not to draw any undue attention to the student you are concerned about.

- Look for strategies the student may be using to support their speech, language or communication skills, such as using peers as a source of information; their ability to ask for information or clarification; and making use of any visual information available.

- Work together to achieve a full picture of a student's needs:
    - gather historical information
    - discuss the information already known
    - agree where, when and how the observations will take place
    - identify strengths and needs
    - ask the student for his/her views
    - involve parents
    - ask other practitioners in school for their views
    - agree how information will be shared.

- Move forward:
    - share the findings as a team
    - make sense of the findings using the Language for Learning model of speech, language and communication skills described in Chapter 2
    - decide what to do next
    - choose appropriate strategies, as suggested in Chapter 5.

Outside Agency Involvement

It may be necessary to involve outside agencies such as speech and language therapists, educational psychologists or specialist teachers at this stage. Outside agencies will be able to help school practitioners to identify:

- SLCN much more specifically, through the use of formalised assessments;

- specific strengths within speech, language or communication;

- hidden receptive language difficulties that may not be apparent through observation;

- SLCN in the context of the student's other skills and abilities, such as whether SLCN is related to a learning difficulty or a primary, specific SLCN;

- any associated behaviour, social and emotional needs.

Observation-based Identification Tools

The identification tools provided in this chapter have been designed to help practitioners to make sense of their observations by making links to the Language for Learning model of speech, language and communication skills described in Chapter 2. They are designed to be quick and easy to complete and will lead directly to target setting and strategy planning.

1 The 'Key Indicators of SLCN' tool on page 35 provides practitioners with the opportunity to record information about an individual student or a whole year group. A list of key indicators of SLCN is provided against each area of language. As difficulties are observed, the practitioner can record students' names or comment on individual students' needs. This tool is useful as an initial screen for SLCN and as an efficient way of sharing information between year group teachers.

2 The 'Observation-based Assessment' tool on page 37 takes a more detailed look at all speech, language and communication skills, reminding practitioners of specific areas to observe and consider. Practitioners can use existing knowledge of the student to answer each question by ticking the yes/ no column and adding any additional comments. Ticks in the 'no' column suggest potential areas of difficulty. This tool can be given to subject teachers to complete to gain a picture of a student's skills across curriculum areas.

3 The 'Observation Record Sheet' on page 40 is an open recording sheet allowing practitioners to record observations over a period of time within each area of language. A profile can be formed by recording strengths and needs within each area. Additional considerations are listed on the second page.

4   The 'Student's Feedback' form on page 41 provides the opportunity for students to give each subject a score based on either their feelings of the subject, e.g. whether they enjoy it or not or based on their confidence (i.e. whether they feel confident in the subject or not). You can choose whether to ask students to rate their feelings or confidence. Depending on the student's awareness and willingness to be open, this tool may help to pinpoint issues with specific subjects and can lead to further discussion about subjects that are at either end of the scale, e.g. 'What makes you feel confident in history?'; 'What makes science difficult?'. You may choose to take a closer look at those subjects that are problematic for a student by utilising the language-friendly environment audit tools in Chapter 4.

5   The 'Student's Skills' rating scale on page 42 asks students to rate their own speech, language and communication skills. Many students with SLCN will have an awareness of their SLCN and some will be able to discuss their needs openly, describing the specific difficulties they experience in school. This scale acts as a starting point and can be used to open a discussion about the difficulties the student is experiencing. Depending on the student's understanding of language and literacy skills, you may need to simplify or adapt this scale to ensure a reliable response.

6   The 'Information from Parents' record sheet on page 43 is a very simple information sheet to gather information from parents regarding their child's strengths and needs at home. This can be used as a discussion point when meeting parents as part of the assessment process.

1 Key Indicators of SLCN

Student:				Date:

Year group:				

AREA	INDICATOR	YES	NO	COMMENTS/EXAMPLES/NAMES
	Difficulties sustaining attention and listening			
	Appears to lack motivation and interest			
	More able to engage when visually supported			
	Easily distracted			
	Limited or weak vocabulary skills			
	Difficulties generalising and using new vocabulary			
	Difficulties with abstract concepts			
	Confused by words with multiple meanings			
	Difficulties defining or demonstrating understanding of the meaning of vocabulary			
	Word-finding difficulties			
	Makes grammatical errors			
	Struggles to sequence ideas and organise information			
	Weak sound knowledge/ awareness of vocabulary			

AREA	INDICATOR	YES	NO	COMMENTS/EXAMPLES/NAMES
	Difficulties understanding/ applying social rules			
	Difficulties using language flexibly			
	Difficulties maintaining a conversation			
	Difficulties with non-verbal communication			
	Inappropriate classroom and social behaviour			
	Makes literal interpretations, does not understand jokes, sarcasm, idioms, ambiguity			
	Forgetful, does not remember			
	Difficulties with long, complex instructions, despite listening			
	Gets lost within activities			
	Unclear or unintelligible speech			
	Lacks fluency when speaking			
	Struggles to assimilate and make sense of information			
	Difficulties using language to reason, predict and make inferences			
	Lacks organisational skills			

2 Observation-based Assessment

Student:			Date:	

Year group:				

AREA	YES	NO	COMMENTS/EXAMPLES
Attention and Listening Skills			
1. Does the student demonstrate appropriate attention and listening skills during: • individual work with an adult or a peer? • small-group work? • whole-class work?			
2. Does he/she respond appropriately during: • small-group work? • whole-class situations?			
3. Does he/she respond appropriately to: • instructions? • questions? • discussions/general conversation?			
4. Does he/she ask for clarification or seek additional information?			
Understanding the Meaning of Words			
5. Does he/she use vocabulary appropriately across situations?			
6. Is he/she able to learn and retrieve subject-based vocabulary demonstrating understanding and appropriate use across situations?			
7. Is he/she able to learn and use abstract concepts, demonstrating understanding?			

AREA	YES	NO	COMMENTS/EXAMPLES
8. Is he/she able to define words clearly?			
9. Is he/she able to understand questions, e.g. 'when', 'why' and 'how'?			
Structure and Rules			
10. Is he/she able to construct sentences using appropriate grammar?			
11. Does he/she use the correct word order when constructing sentences?			
12. Is he/she able to sequence and order information, e.g. with a beginning, middle and end?			
13. Does he/she re-tell a story or an event in the correct order?			
14. Does he/she demonstrate sound awareness/knowledge of vocabulary?			
Social Communication Skills			
15. Does the student use his/her language skills for a range of reasons?			
16. Is he/she able to initiate and maintain a conversation?			
17. Does he/she stay on topic?			
18. Is he/she able to develop a conversation beyond one or two turns?			
19. Does he/she demonstrate an understanding and appropriate use of non-verbal communication skills?			
20. Does he/she provide sufficient information for a listener to understand?			

AREA	YES	NO	COMMENTS/EXAMPLES
21. Does he/she recognise and then clarify any misunderstandings?			
22. Does he/she give relevant responses?			
23. Does he/she adapt language use according to the situation and conversational partner?			
Working Auditory Memory			
24. Does the student remember information presented verbally, such as instructions and information?			
25. Is he/she able to relay messages accurately?			
26. Does he/she remember instructions related to homework or equipment?			
Speech			
27. Is he/she able to speak clearly, producing speech sounds accurately?			
Thinking Skills			
28. Does the student use his/her language skills for complex functions, e.g. to reason, predict, make inferences?			
29. Is he/she able to use language to imagine?			
30. Does he/she express feelings in words?			

3 Observation Record Sheet

Student:	Year Group:	
Practitioner:	Timescale:	

CONTEXTS OBSERVED:

Attention and Listening Skills

Understanding the Meaning of Words

Structure and Rules

Social Communication Skills

Working Auditory Memory

Speech

Thinking Skills

History of speech, language or communication needs:

Preferred learning style:

General learning ability:

Organisational skills:

Hobbies/interests:

Relationships in school:

Strengths:

Feedback/comments from parents:

4 Student's Feedback

Student:	Year group:	Date:

EITHER Give each subject a score from 1–4: 4 = I really enjoy it 1 = I don't enjoy it		OR Give each subject a score from 1–4: 4 = I feel really confident 1 = I feel under confident		
SUBJECT	☹			☺
	1	**2**	**3**	**4**
English				
Maths				
Science				
History				
Geography				
Religious education				
Modern foreign languages, e.g. French				
Music				
Art and design				
Design and technology				
ICT				
PSHEE				
Citizenship				
Other:				

5 Student's Skills

Student:	Year group:	Date:

Think about your skills and give each skill a score from 1–4:

    4 = I am very good at this

    1 = I find this very difficult

SKILLS	☹			☺
	1	**2**	**3**	**4**
Listening in class				
Staying focused				
Understanding what to do in lessons				
Answering questions				
Learning new words				
Explaining what words mean				
Telling a story				
Telling someone about something that has happened				
Joining in with discussions in class				
Having a conversation				
Understanding jokes				
Working in groups				
Keeping up in fast conversations				
Remembering homework				
Remembering equipment				
Remembering what to do in lessons				
Speaking in class				
Speaking to my friends				

6 Information from Parents

Student:	Year group:	Date:

Parent's name and contact details:

PLEASE COMMENT ON:	
Your child's communication skills at home:	
Your child's ability to understand at home, e.g. following instructions, understanding jokes or sarcasm, understanding plots on TV:	
Social skills:	
Being organised for school, including homework:	
Your child's favourite activities:	
Any speech, language or communication difficulties experienced in the past:	

4 A Whole-School Approach

A whole-school approach is both an efficient and effective way to support students with speech, language and communication needs in your school. Working as a team not only ensures consistency and progression, it also fosters the sharing of knowledge and skills, avoiding duplication. All members of the school team need to be included so students have maximum opportunities to learn and generalise skills across school contexts and at home.

A whole-school approach will include: leaders (the school's senior management team), SEN governor, SEN co-ordinator, heads of year, heads of departments, teachers, teaching assistants (TAs), administrative staff, lunchtime supervisors (LTS) and, of course, students and parents.

This chapter aims to support your school in achieving a whole-school approach by considering SLCN initiatives, the role and responsibilities of staff, parents and students and being aware of the challenges and opportunities within subject areas.

'Roles and Responsibilities', starting on page 46, identifies the reader's role and links it to SLCN initiatives, skills, responsibilities and the roles of others. It also suggests relevant information and materials, some of which are included in this book; others are readily obtainable through the DFE and national organisations.

KEY TO COLOUR CODING AND ABBREVIATIONS	
Senior management team	LEADERS
SEN co-ordinator	SENCO
Parents	PARENTS
Students	STUDENTS
Heads of year	HEADS OF YEAR
Heads of departments	HEADS OF DEPTS
Teachers	TEACHERS
Teaching assistants	TAS
Lunchtime supervisors	LTS
Administration assistants	ADMINS
SEN governor	SEN GOVS

'Opportunities and Challenges', the most significant of these starting on page 78, considers each subject area and links the key opportunities and challenges to possible solutions. These solutions are grouped in the Language for Learning language areas and linked to specific, numbered strategies all located in Chapter 5. To understand challenges further, a list of observed behaviours can be found at the beginning of each language area in Chapter 5.

The *Literacy in...* series (DFE standards website) suggests ideas for teaching speaking and listening within all curriculum subjects.

All publications referred to are fully referenced in the bibliography on pages 141–142.

Roles and Responsibilities

LEADERS

INITIATIVES	SKILLS AND KNOWLEDGE	WHO
1 Enhance the learning and social opportunities for all students within your school by supporting SLCN initiatives	• Good understanding of SLCN • Understanding of the link between SLCN and the specific environmental and social factors of the school's catchment area. • Awareness of potential issues for students with SLCN. • Awareness of how language skills affect the management and regulation of emotions. • Understanding the link between SLCN and behavioural, emotional and social development. • Remembering that inclusive SLCN provision enhances the learning of most students.	SENCO
2 SLCN awareness and general strategy training	• Familiar with current national initiatives and research.	SENCO HEADS OF YEAR HEADS OF DEPTS TEACHERS TAS
3 Whole-school audit of SLCN knowledge of universal strategies	• Support the implementation of whole-school provision for SLCN.	
4 Development of a whole-school approach	• An understanding that the challenges facing students with SLCN in the secondary school are best addressed with consistency and team work. • Awareness of the specific difficulties for students with SLCN during the times of transition.	EVERYONE
5 Measure outcomes	• Ability to interpret information from school audit.	SENCO

LEADERS

ROLE	INFORMATION	TOOL BOX
1 Encourage a whole-school approach, sign up to national associations and prioritise training to enhance your SENCO's knowledge and skills. Liaise with outside agencies, e.g. the Speech and Language Therapy Service, Specialist Teacher Service, Educational Psychology and those working with students who are suspended or permanently excluded.	Chapter 4, page 44 Organisations: Department for Education AFASIC National Association for Special Educational Needs (NASEN) The Communication Trust National Association for Practitioners working with Language Impairment in Children (NAPLIC)	*Speech Language and Communication Framework (The Communication Trust)* *Inclusion Development Plan (DCSF)* *Don't Get Me Wrong (The Communication Trust)* *Sentence Trouble (The Communication Trust)*
2 Prioritise training allowing time for planning and embedding practice.	SENCO	Training handouts
3 Oversee audit, working with SENCO.	'Identification Tools', pages 33–43	'Identification Tools', pages 33–43 'Developing a Language-Friendly Environment', pages 67–71
4 Implement as part of whole-school policy building in team work, consistency and progression.	Chapters 4 and 5, pages 44–136 'Consistency Across the School', page 72	'Developing a Language-Friendly Environment' pages 67–71
5 Incorporate SLCN outcomes into teacher observations.	SENCO	'Developing a Language-Friendly Environment' pages 67–71

SENCO

INITIATIVES	SKILLS AND KNOWLEDGE	WHO
1 Speech, language and communication needs awareness training for all staff	• Understanding of SLCN. • Knowledge of potential issues for students with SLCN. • Familiar with the SLCF. • Good training skills.	**LEADERS** HEADS OF YEAR HEADS OF DEPTS **TEACHERS TAS**
2 Knowledge of universal strategies	• Knowledge of general strategies and resources for use at a universal level.	
3 Whole-school audit of SLCN	• Ability to identify need (staff and pupils), plan, provision and measure outcomes.	
4 Development of a language-friendly environment	• An understanding of the challenges facing students with SLCN in the secondary school and how the school environment has an impact.	
5 Provision for targeted and specialist support	• Knowledge of specific strategies and resources.	**TEACHERS TAS**
6 TA lesson knowledge	• Managing curriculum information.	
7 Developing student independence	• Encouraging students to take responsibility for their learning.	**STUDENTS**
8 Good links between school and home	• An ability to include parents as part of the school's support team.	PARENTS
9 Good transition between primary and secondary	• An understanding of the challenges facing pupils with SLCN during periods of transition. • Knowledge of successful strategies.	HEADS OF YEAR
10 Good transition from year to year		
11 Development of departmental, subject-specific strategies and resources	• An understanding of how resources can be adapted to make them curriculum friendly. • Knowledge of the opportunities and challenges in a range of subject areas.	HEADS OF DEPTS
12 Reinforcement of universal strategies at lunchtime	• Knowledge of the issues facing students with SLCN during the lunch break.	LTS

ROLE	INFORMATION	TOOL BOX
1 Encourage a whole-school approach to identification, strategies and resources.	All Chapters Local SLT and SEN services DFE and national organisations	*Speech Language and Communication Framework* (The Communication Trust) *Inclusion Development Plan* *Don't Get Me Wrong* (The Communication Trust) *Sentence Trouble* (The Communication Trust)
2 Build in consistency – use universal strategies throughout the school.	Chapter 4 Chapter 5	
3 Manage information recorded by teachers, TAs and parents.	Chapter 3	'Identification Tools', pages 33–43
4 Implement as part of whole-school policy. Provide guidelines for non-teaching staff.	Chapter 4	'Developing a Language-Friendly Environment', pages 67–71
5 Discuss and demonstrate specific strategies.	Local SLT and SEN services	A demonstration pack of resources
6 Work with teachers to ensure that TAs know lesson content in advance.	'Developing Language-friendly Environments', pages 67–71	Lesson plans Revision guides Vocabulary lists
7 Ensure that students work towards using strategies independently.	'Developing Independence', pages 73–4	'Record of Support', pages 76–7
8 Gather information and discuss strategies, resources, visual timetable and homework.	School's homework guidelines	'Information from Parents', page 43. Chapter 5 – At Home Strategies Student's visual timetable
9 Take time to liaise between schools and develop information packs.	*Transition to Secondary School* (TCT) *Transfer to Secondary School* (AFASIC) *Talking About Secondary School* (Black Sheep Press)	School's transition pack
10 Be consistent, pass on identification sheets, continue using strategies.	'Consistency Across the School', page 72	'Identification Tools', pages 33–43
11 Support heads of departments to establish working parties to make resources subject-specific.	'Introducing Strategies', page 98 'Working within Your Department', page 75 'Adapting Resources', page 73	Resource examples
12 Train LTS to use social skills strategies. Provide materials.	Chapter 5	A demonstration pack of resources

PARENTS

INITIATIVES	SKILLS AND KNOWLEDGE	WHO
1 SLCN training	• Desire to know more about your child's SLCN. • The wealth of knowledge you already have about SLCN.	SENCO
2 Awareness of all strategies being used with your child at school	• A willingness to become involved with support in school.	SENCO TAS
3 General support at home to develop useful skills	• The belief that it is possible to make a difference.	SENCO TEACHERS TAS
4 Good home–school liaison	• Confidence to share your knowledge and understanding of your child's needs and effective support strategies. • Have a consistent approach to communication with school.	
5 Transition from primary to secondary and from year to year	• Sharing what you know about your child with secondary school staff. • Weighing up the school's reputation for SLCN with other factors such as distance from home, friendship groups, out-of-school activities.	SENCO HEADS OF YEAR TAS

PARENTS

ROLE	INFORMATION	TOOL BOX
1 Accept training on offer in school. Investigate training opportunities within your authority. Go to national organisations online.	Consult SENCO AFASIC, NASEN, The Communication Trust, NAPLIC contact details, page 142	Training handouts
2 Discuss strategies with your child's SENCO, teacher or TA. Offer to reinforce at home. Accept resources supplied by school to help.	Chapter 5, page 97	Resources supplied by school
3 Use the 'At Home' strategy sheets to support your child's skills development. Introduce your child to the vocabulary of forthcoming topics.	Chapter 5, page 97 Discuss with TA, teacher or SENCO	Chapter 5 'At Home strategies' Topic vocabulary lists
4 Seek opportunities to meet with school staff to share information. Use the school's homework guidelines. Support your child to use his/her visual timetable.	*Coaching Your Teenager* Department for Education, page 141	School's homework guidelines Child's visual timetable
5 Take opportunities to visit your chosen secondary school during Years 5 and 6 (social situations are good). Go through the school's transition pack with your child regularly before he or she starts. Find out what is different about the next year and prepare your child in advance.	*Transition to Secondary School* (TCT) *Transfer to Secondary School* (AFASIC)	School's transition pack

STUDENTS

INITIATIVES	SKILLS AND KNOWLEDGE	WHO
1 Awareness of strengths and weaknesses	• Desire to know more about who you are. • Knowing that everyone is different and that everyone finds something challenging.	SENCO PARENTS TAS
2 Learning helpful strategies	• A willingness to try out and work at strategies that may help you to learn and/or make friends more easily.	SENCO TAS
3 Using strategies in a variety of situations	• Accepting that strategies learned to support the ability to do something may be useful in a lot of other situations.	SENCO PARENTS TAS
4 Learning to take control	• Wanting to become independent. • A willingness to work on organisational skills. • Developing your listening skills. • Taking responsibility for not understanding.	SENCO PARENTS TEACHERS TAS
5 Transition from primary to secondary and from year to year	• Being curious about the next move and wanting to find out more so that you will be prepared.	SENCO HEADS OF YEAR PARENTS TAS

STUDENTS

ROLE	INFORMATION	TOOL BOX
1 Think about the things you find easy and those you find difficult in different subjects and situations in school. Share this information with the teachers and TAs you work with. Talk to your family.	Parents Other family members *Talking Point* (AFASIC), page 142	'Student's Feedback', page 41 'Student's Summary of Skills', page 42 'Developing a Language-Friendly Environment', Student View, pages 67–71
2 Have a go at using strategies suggested by teachers, TAs and your parents – they could work well for you. Accept that this may take a bit of hard work to start with and may not go exactly to plan but could be GREAT in the long run.	SENCO Teachers TAs Parents	Resources provided
3 Discuss the strategies you like best with your TA or teacher and together adapt them for situations out of school. Get your family involved.	Chapter 5, page 97	Chapter 5, 'At Home strategies'
4 Try to do things by yourself using the strategies you have become familiar with. Ask for help when you have not understood something or you are not sure what to do next. Talk to adults you get on with about friendship issues.	Chapter 5, page 97	'Task-Management Boards', page 102 'Visual Timetables', page 101 'Visual Dictionaries', page 111 'Personal Word Books', page 111 'Mind Maps', page 110
5 Take opportunities to visit your secondary school during Years 5 and 6 (social situations are good). Go through the school's transition pack with your family regularly before you start your new school to become familiar with it. Take photos when you visit so that you remember key people and places in the school. Try to meet other students who live near you before you go. Ask another student or a TA to tell you what is different about the following year and to show you unfamiliar places.	AFASIC NASEN TCT	'Transition Checklist for Students with SLCN', pages 65–6 School's transition pack

HEADS OF YEAR

INITIATIVES	SKILLS AND KNOWLEDGE	WHO
1 Enhance the learning and social opportunities for all pupils within your year group by supporting SLCN initiatives	• Good understanding of SLCN. • Awareness of potential issues for pupils with SLCN. • Awareness of how language skills affect the management and regulation of emotions. • Remembering that inclusive SLCN provision enhances the learning of most pupils. • Understanding the link between SLCN and behavioural, emotional and social development.	SENCO
2 Development of a language-friendly environment	• Open to training opportunities. • Managing consistent use of strategies in your year.	SENCO HEADS OF DEPTS TEACHERS TAS
3 Whole-school audit of SLCN; knowledge of universal strategies	• Overview of the needs in your year.	
4 Good transition from primary to secondary (Head of Year 7)	• An understanding of the challenges facing pupils with SLCN as they move to a new environment.	LEADERS SENCO TEACHERS TAS
5 Good transition from year to year	• An understanding of the challenges facing pupils with SLCN during times of transition.	SENCO HEADS OF DEPTS TEACHERS TAS

ROLE	INFORMATION	TOOL BOX
1 Attend training opportunities offered to staff in your year and support the implementation of strategies.	Pages 141–42 AFASIC NASEN The Communication Trust NAPLIC	*Speech Language & Communication Framework* (SLCF) *Don't Get Me Wrong* (The Communication Trust) *Inclusion Development Programme* (IDP)
2 Prioritise training, allowing time for planning and embedding practice.		Training handouts
3 Support your SENCO by working with the staff in your year to gather data and pass information on to the next year head.		'Identification Tools', pages 33–43 'Developing a Language-Friendly Environment', pages 67–71
4 Liaise between schools, arrange staff and student visits and set up information packs.	*Transition to Secondary School* (TCT) *Transfer to Secondary School* (AFASIC)	School's transition pack
5 Oversee consistent use of strategies and resources building in progression as students move from one year to another. Pass on observations and strategy history.		'Developing a Language-Friendly Environment', pages 67–71 'Record of Support', pages 76–7 'Consistency Across the School', page 72

HEADS OF YEAR

HEADS OF DEPTS

INITIATIVES	SKILLS AND KNOWLEDGE	WHO
1 Enhance the learning and social opportunities for all students within your department by supporting SLCN initiatives	• Good understanding of SLCN. • Awareness of potential issues for students with SLCN. • Awareness of how language skills affect the management and regulation of emotions. • Remembering that inclusive SLCN provision enhances the learning of most students. • Understanding the link between SLCN and behavioural, emotional and social development.	SENCO
2 Development of a language-friendly environment	• Open to training opportunities. • Knowledge of universal strategies. • Awareness of targeted and specialist strategies. • Management of the use of strategies in your department.	SENCO HEADS OF YEAR TEACHERS TAS
3 Whole-school audit of SLCN	• Overview of the needs in your department. • Awareness that a 'whole-school approach' for SLCN works well. • For all young people.	LEADERS SENCO TEACHERS TAS
4 Development of departmental, subject-specific strategies and resources	• An understanding of the opportunities and challenges within your subject for students with SLCN. • An overview of vocabulary and concepts being taught. • Management of resources.	SENCO HEADS OF YEAR TEACHERS TAS

ROLE	INFORMATION	TOOL BOX
1 Attend training opportunities offered to staff in your department and support the implementation of strategies.	Pages 141–42 AFASIC NASEN The Communication Trust NAPLIC	*Speech, Language & Communication Framework* (The Communication Trust) *Don't Get Me Wrong* (The Communication Trust) *Inclusion Development Programme* (IDP)
2 Prioritise training, allowing time for planning and embedding practice. Encourage teachers to use good communication strategies for whole-class teaching monitoring during teacher observations. Support strategy use – consider consistency and progression.	Chapters 1, 2 and 3 'Introducing Strategies', page 98 'Consistency Across the School', page 72 Chapter 5	Training handouts 'Developing a Language-Friendly Environment', pages 67–71
3 Support your SENCO by working with the staff in your department to gather data.	Chapter 3	'Identification Tools', pages 33–43 'Language-Friendly Environment Tools', pages 67–71
4 Support your SENCO by providing lesson plans and vocabulary lists to TAs well in advance of lessons. Work with your staff to develop curriculum-friendly resources, avoiding duplication and creating an easy-access storage system.	'Working within your Department', page 75	A demonstration pack of resources

HEADS OF DEPTS

TEACHERS

INITIATIVES	SKILLS AND KNOWLEDGE	WHO
1 Speech, language and communication needs awareness training	• Understanding of SLCN. • Knowledge of potential issues for pupils with SLCN. • Familiar with the SLCF. • Awareness of how language skills affect the management and regulation of behaviour and emotions. • Understanding the link between SLCN and behavioural, emotional and social development. • Remembering that inclusive SLCN provision enhances the learning of most pupils.	SENCO HEADS OF YEAR HEADS OF DEPTS TAS
2 Whole-school audit of SLCN	• Ability to identify students' needs, plan, provision and measure outcomes.	
3 Development of a language-friendly environment	• Knowledge of a range of universal strategies and resources. • An understanding of the challenges facing students with SLCN in the secondary school.	
4 Working in partnership with TAs	• An understanding of the challenges facing TAs. • Knowledge of the specific needs of the students they work with.	TAS
5 Development of departmental, subject-specific strategies and resources	• An understanding of how resources can be adapted to make them curriculum-friendly. • Knowledge of the opportunities and challenges in a range of subject areas.	HEADS OF DEPTS
6 Developing student independence	• Encouraging students to take responsibility for their learning. • Supporting TAs when they are encouraging students to become independent.	STUDENTS TAS
7 Good links between school and home	• Accepting that parents know their children well, their view is important and sharing ideas benefits everyone. • An ability to keep parents included and informed.	PARENTS

TEACHERS

ROLE	INFORMATION	TOOL BOX
1 Take training opportunities. Take responsibility for putting theory into practice. Adapt and monitor your communication skills.	Chapters 1–3 The Communication Trust AFASIC NASEN NAPLIC	*Speech Language & Communication Framework* (The Communication Trust) *Don't Get Me Wrong* (The Communication Trust) 'Developing a Language-Friendly Environment', pages 67–71
2 Record observations of students' SLCN, sharing data with other staff.		'Identification Tools', pages 33–43
3 Consider your role in the development of your students' speech, language and communication skills and their ability to make relationships.	Training handouts Chapters 1, 2 and 3	'Developing a Language-Friendly Environment', pages 67–71
4 Support TAs by reinforcing strategies within the classroom and providing lesson plans and vocabulary lists in advance of topics. Arrange time to plan together and discuss students' needs.		Liaison sheets Lesson plans Vocabulary lists Revision guides
5 Develop resources that are curriculum friendly. Work together as a department dividing the work and sharing rather than duplicating and store for ease of access.	'Opportunities and Challenges', pages 78–96 'Adapting Resources', page 73 'Working within your Department', page 75 Chapter 5 – commercial resources (for inspiration)	Examples
6 Take time to teach strategies, adapting to suit the individual and building in consistency and progression. Ensure that students work towards using strategies independently.	Chapter 5 'Introducing Strategies', page 98 'Consistency Across the School', page 72 'Developing Independence', pages 73–4	'Student's Feedback', page 41 'Student's Summary of Skills', page 42 'Developing a Language-Friendly Environment – Student Views', page 70 'Record of Support', page 76
7 Discuss and complete the 'Information from Parents' sheet and decide how you are going to work together. Provide resources. Provide consistent support for understanding and completing homework.	SENCO	'Information from Parents', page 43 'Record of Support', page 76 Chapter 5, 'At Home Strategies', School's homework guidelines

TAS

INITIATIVES	SKILLS AND KNOWLEDGE	WHO
1 Speech, language and communication needs awareness training	• Understanding of SLCN. • Familiar with the SLCF. • Awareness of how language skills affect the management and regulation of behaviour and emotions. • Understanding the link between SLCN and behavioural, emotional and social development.	SENCO
2 Whole-school audit of SLCN	• Ability to observe students and record findings accurately.	TEACHERS
3 Development of a language-friendly environment	• Knowledge of a range of universal strategies and resources. • An understanding of the challenges facing students with SLCN in the secondary school. • Ability to talk to students about what is hard and what is easy for them in school.	STUDENTS
4 Working in partnership with teachers	• An understanding of the challenges facing teachers in the classroom. • An ability to support students inclusively.	TEACHERS
5 Development of departmental, subject-specific strategies and resources	• An understanding of how resources can be adapted to make them curriculum-friendly. • Supporting a system for storing, sharing and accessing resources.	HEADS OF DEPTS TEACHERS
6 Developing student independence	• Ability to encourage students to take responsibility for their learning. • Ability to foster independent use of strategies. • Ability to work with a group of students.	STUDENTS TAS
7 Good links between school and home	• An ability to keep parents included and informed.	PARENTS

TAS

ROLE	INFORMATION	TOOL BOX
1 Take training opportunities. Take responsibility for putting theory into practice. Adapt and monitor your communication skills.	Chapters 1, 2 and 3 SLCF, IDP, National Organisations	Training handouts 'Developing a Language-Friendly Environment', pages 67–71
2 Record observations of students' SLCN, sharing data with teachers and SENCO.	Chapter 3	'Identification Tools', pages 33–43
3 Develop students' ability to listen; process instructions and information; understand the meaning of words and sentences; express their thoughts and feelings and make relationships. Support their ability to remember what they have to do and what they have been taught.	Chapter 5	'Developing a Language-Friendly Environment', pages 67–71
4 Prepare for lessons in advance, consider vocabulary, visual materials and student organisation.	SENCO Heads of departments Teachers	Liaison sheets Lesson plans Vocabulary lists Revision guides
5 Develop resources that are curriculum friendly, using topic vocabulary. Work together within the department, sharing ideas and workload rather than duplicating. Store for ease of access.	'Opportunities and Challenges', pages 78–96 'Adapting Resources', page 73 'Working Within Your Department', page 75 Chapter 5 – commercial resources (for inspiration)	Vocabulary lists Revision guides Commercial resources
6 Take time to teach strategies, adapting to suit the individual and building in consistency and progression. Ensure that students work towards using strategies independently. Check strategy history.	Chapter 5 'Introducing Strategies', page 98 'Consistency Across the School', page 72 'Developing Independence', pages 73–4	Record of Support, page 76
7 Discuss the use of a home–school link book with the SENCO or teacher(s) you work with. Provide consistent support for understanding and completing homework.	Chapter 5	Home–school link book, page 123 Homework support plan

LTS

INITIATIVES	SKILLS AND KNOWLEDGE	WHO
1 Basic awareness of speech language and communication needs	• Willingness to attend training by SENCO. • An understanding of the link between SLCN and behavioural, emotional and social behaviour.	SENCO
2 Reinforcement of a selection of universal strategies at lunchtime	• Ability to use a selection of universal strategies appropriately.	

ADMINS

INITIATIVES	SKILLS AND KNOWLEDGE	WHO
1 Awareness of the whole-school approach to SLCN	• Ability to communicate effectively with SLCN students.	SENCO

SEN GOVS

INITIATIVES	SKILLS AND KNOWLEDGE	WHO
1 Awareness of speech language and communication needs	• Willingness to participate in training.	LEADERS SENCO
2 Awareness of SLCN initiatives prioritised by school leaders and SENCO	• Awareness of national guidelines underpinning school initiatives. • Support school staff with implementation.	
3 Awareness of SLCN audit	• Understanding why this is important and what the benefits will be.	SENCO

ROLE	INFORMATION	TOOL BOX
1 Learn how to communicate with students who have SLCN. Understand the challenges they face during the lunch hour.	SENCO – training	Handout sheets
2 Learn to use strategies to help students develop their language and communication skills and to reinforce what is being done in the classroom and at home.	SENCO	'Active Listening Cue Cards', page 101 'Social Communication Skills Prompts', page 124

ROLE	INFORMATION	TOOL BOX
1 Support students with SLCN by following guidelines from SENCO. Be aware of the roles and responsibilities of staff, parents and students.	SENCO 'Roles and Responsibilities', pages 46–63	Guidelines

ROLE	INFORMATION	TOOL BOX
1 Join in with training and supporting theory into practice by helping at a practical level.	All chapters	Training handouts
2 Discuss initiatives with school leaders and read literature produced by national organisations. Offer practical support.	AFASIC NASEN The Communication Trust	*SLCF* (The Communication Trust) *IDP* *Don't Get Me Wrong* (The Communication Trust) *Sentence Trouble* (The Communication Trust)
3 Discuss findings with leaders to support forward planning.	SENCO	Summary of SLCN needs

Roles and Responsibility Tools

The following are all referenced within the preceding roles and responsibility pages.

1   The 'Transition Checklist for Students with SLCN' on pages 65–6 is a useful list of considerations for parents, primary school staff and secondary school staff.

2   A set of 'Language-Friendly Environment Tools' can be found on pages 67–71 and include:

a   adult communication and classroom practice

b   providing visual support

c   student views

d   developing a skilled workforce.

These tools can be used as a checklist by individual teachers monitoring their own practice or as observation record sheets as part of an audit of whole-school or departmental practice. The 'Student's Views' elicits feedback from individual students in relation to language-friendly strategies and approaches.

Additional information, considerations and tips can be found as below:

3   'Consistency Across the School' on page 72.

4   'Adapting Resources' on pages 73–4.

5   'Developing Independence' on pages 73–4.

6   'Working Within Your Department' on page 75.

7   'Record of Support' on page 76.

1 TRANSITION CHECKLIST for STUDENTS with SLCN

HOME – How to prepare your son/daughter

Use home visual timetables and set up an evening routine to include homework and getting things ready for the next day (see p. 101)	
Practice using plans in shopping malls and town centres	
Organisation: provide a place to work and to keep school clothes and containers to store school equipment, books and work	
Find out about the colour coding used in secondary school and start using it at home to mark books and add to visual timetables	
Discuss the things that your son/daughter will like about their new school	
Practice doing activities for the same length of time as your son/daughter's lessons will be	
Familiarise your son/daughter with the journey to school	
Discuss issues to do with going to the toilet and illness at school	
Discuss the school rules – what they mean and how they are kept	
Make a pictorial folder for their new school include information about family and pets, interests, strengths and weaknesses, likes and dislikes, what they are looking forward to and what they are concerned about	

PRIMARY SCHOOL – What to prepare pupils for

Using visual timetables (see p. 101) and homework diaries	
Moving between classrooms	
Working with different teachers during the same day	
Taking responsibility for not understanding	
Asking for and understanding directions	
The names of subjects and other activities in secondary school	
The names of the Head teacher, SENCO, Year 7 teachers and their subjects and TAs (photos if possible)	
Changing for PE quickly	
Make mind maps (see p. 110) of aspects to do with Secondary School	
Make a pictorial folder for their new school include information about family and pets, interests, strengths and weaknesses, likes and dislikes, what they are looking forward to and what they are concerned about	

SECONDARY SCHOOL – What to provide in advance

Examples of visual timetables (see p.101) and homework diaries	
Plans of the school with departments, hall, admin and dining areas clearly marked	
Details of the school day: what happens and when, where lockers are, where coats are left etc.	
Information about lunchtimes and after school clubs	

SECONDARY SCHOOL – What to provide in school

Buddy system – Year 8 students	
Clear signs around the school – (colour coded if possible)	
Name badges to wear or name labels for desks for both students and staff	
List of school rules to primary school and home	
Colour-coded books/subjects and add coding to visual timetables	
Names and photos of key staff – for primary school and home	

PUPIL PROFILE – What to consider

SLCN – Overview of information from any of the 'Language for Learning Identification Tools' (see pp. 33–43)	
Learning style	
Literacy ability	
Emotional literacy	
Flexibility	
Ability to make friends	
Interests	
Health issues & personal hygiene	
Understanding of rules	
Coping with unstructured time	
Response to praise	

2 Language-Friendly Environment Tools

DEVELOPING A LANGUAGE-FRIENDLY ENVIRONMENT

a. Adult communication and classroom practice

Subject Teacher:	Date:		
Skills	**In Use**	**To Develop**	**Review**
Speaks clearly and slowly			
Uses eye contact			
Uses facial expressions			
Uses gesture/signing			
Keeps grammar and vocabulary simple			
Keeps questioning to a minimum; uses commenting and describing to engage with student(s)			
Makes the order of action the order of mention			
Identifies new vocabulary and explains it			
Explains idioms and non-literal language			
Varies teaching style			
Uses objects and pictures to support spoken language			
Reads out what is written on the white board			
Provides clear instructions for homework including 'what', 'when' and 'how'			
Strategies			
Uses active listening p. 101 (17)			
Uses the ten-second rule p. 100 (11)			
Encourages students to take responsibility for not understanding p. 101 (18)			
Positions students so that eye contact can be maintained (student–teacher/student–student)			

Strategies continued	In Use	To Develop	Review
Introduces and controls a variety of noise levels in the classroom			
Provides clear worksheets			
Supports comprehension exercises with colour-coding p. 135 (9)			
Shows finished examples			
Arranges seating so that concentration can be maintained p. 103 (27)			
Equipment			
Use of appropriate equipment to support spoken communication, e.g. recording devices			
Uses talking dictionaries and calculators			
Managing Teaching Assistants			
Is clear about roles and responsibilities			
Shares information about student needs			
Gives positive feedback about TA's work			
Encourages and supports training opportunities			
Instigates regular joint planning opportunities and supplies topic information and vocabulary lists in advance			
Is clear about aims of the lesson and expectations of students' contributions			
Values TA feedback and observations			
Manages TAs time efficiently and effectively; e.g. time teaching a student a strategy for life is more worthwhile than sitting through a lesson that the student can work in independently; TAs' time can be used creatively to support the use of visual information in the classroom with allocated time for resource development			

DEVELOPING A LANGUAGE-FRIENDLY ENVIRONMENT
b. Providing visual support

Methods	Evidence	Action to be taken	Achieved
Staff awareness of visual recognition levels of development			
Clear signage around the school			
Visual support at appropriate eye-level			
Text supported by photos, pictures or symbols			
Visual timetables supplied to students and displayed in classrooms and corridors for lessons and out-of-school clubs			
Classroom strategies supported by appropriate visuals			
Task management boards used when appropriate in all lessons			

DEVELOPING A LANGUAGE-FRIENDLY ENVIRONMENT

c. Student views

Student:		Date:
Subject:		

The teacher ...	☹ Strongly disagree			☺ Strongly agree
	1	**2**	**3**	**4**
... speaks clearly and slowly.				
... communicates well.				
... speaks in sentences that I can understand.				
... uses words that I understand.				
... explains what new words mean.				
... gives good explanations to help us understand.				
... shows us what to do as well as telling us.				
... uses objects, photographs and pictures when talking – this helps us to understand.				
... reads what is written on the board.				
... reminds us of good listening skills.				
... gives us thinking time.				
... encourages us to ask for help or ask questions when we don't understand.				
... uses easy-to-understand worksheets.				

DEVELOPING A LANGUAGE-FRIENDLY ENVIRONMENT

d. Developing a skilled workforce: SLCN training record

Whole school

Department

Individual

Name:

Course Details	SLCN Awareness	Identification Tools	Universal Approaches	Targeted Approaches	Specialised Approaches

3 Consistency across the School

In developing a whole-school approach it is important that attention is given to consistency and progression throughout the school. To maximise opportunities to learn and generalise skills, strategies must be used in a range of contexts. To avoid confusion for students all staff must be consistent in the way they are both introduced and used. Of course, there will be variations on how they are designed to meet the challenges of specific situations and subjects and to cater for individual students' needs. Building in progression is obviously important too – strategies and resources will need to be adapted, increasing expectations and reflecting the students' growing abilities.

Consider the following:

Around the School

- What type of visual support will be used – photographs, pictures, symbols, colour-coding, etc.?
- How will it be displayed – posters, labels, wall charts, cartoon strips, etc.?
- What will it address – helping students to find their way around, information about school activities, information about behaviour, information to do with health and safety, etc.?

Learning Tasks

- What type of visual support will be used – photographs, pictures, symbols, colour-coding, etc.?
- How will consistency be achieved while meeting individual needs?
- How will it be adapted for specific subjects?
- Who will be responsible for the 'corporate' design and style?
- How will developmental progression be ensured?
- How will ideas be shared?
- How will resources be shared and accessed?

Targeted Intervention

- How will strategies taught in small, targeted interventions (e.g. social communication skills groups) be reinforced in the classroom, the wider school and at home?

4 Adapting Resources

There are many resources on the market to address the needs of young children with SLCN, but far fewer for older students. However, many games and activities designed for the younger child are easily adaptable for secondary-aged students.

Consider the following:

- Take inspiration from traditional board and card games as well as those designed for younger students.

- Make the game short so it can be played at the end of an activity or lesson – little and often is the best way to develop skills and reinforce vocabulary.

- Use subject-specific vocabulary and pictures but share the game concept with other departments so skills are transferred across contexts.

- Take advantage of the social opportunities games create, developing social communication skills such as turn-taking and developing peer relationships.

- Store for ease of access and opportunity to share. Leave directions with the resource and encourage colleagues to add their adaptations.

5 Developing Independence

In secondary school, students are expected to be organised and independent. This can be challenging for many students, but for those with SLCN the difficulties are wide-ranging as a student may:

- experience difficulties with sequential thinking and organisational skills;

- struggle to follow verbal instructions and remember what to do;

- not have the skills to make use of strategies such as timetables or planners.

There is little time spent providing visual support, making expectations clear or practising these skills. It is important, therefore, to create opportunities to teach these skills and reinforce them in every context possible.

Consider the following:

- Expectations – how will consistency across the school and progression from year to year be ensured?

- Time issues – how will students with SLCN be taught and supported to get to school and lessons on time, pace their work during lessons, understand the bell system and cope with forward planning for long-term assignments?

- Materials and equipment – what support will SLCN students be given to select the correct equipment for the task in hand, bring what they need to every lesson and know what they will need to complete homework?

- What will happen about their work – how will they store and access it?

- Directions – what provision will be made to ensure that students can find their way around the school?

- Homework – how will SLCN students understand and record homework information and know when to hand it in?

- Communication – how will support be given so that notices, changes in routine and activity opportunities are communicated to students with SLCN?

Some useful strategies and resources include:

- Visual timetables (see page 101, strategy 19).

- Visual timelines – a strip placed around the form room with main events marked, including assignment dates and an arrow pinpointing 'today' (see page 111, strategy 18).

- Task-management boards (see page 102, strategy 21).

- Diaries – ensure that students know how to make best use of them. Use coloured pens for different tasks/events, e.g. red for after-school activities, blue for equipment, green for homework, etc. Include information that the student may forget, such as names of teachers, tables, quantities, spellings for days of the week, months of the year, etc.

- Colour-coding for directions and subject areas, such as classroom doors, text books, files and folders, etc.

- Plastic wallets, concertina files, page dividers, etc. – assign an adult to support regular 'tidying' of work, lockers, etc.

6 Working within Your Department

Create opportunities within your department to foster speech, language and communication development. Remember that inclusive provision for SLCN enhances the learning of most students.

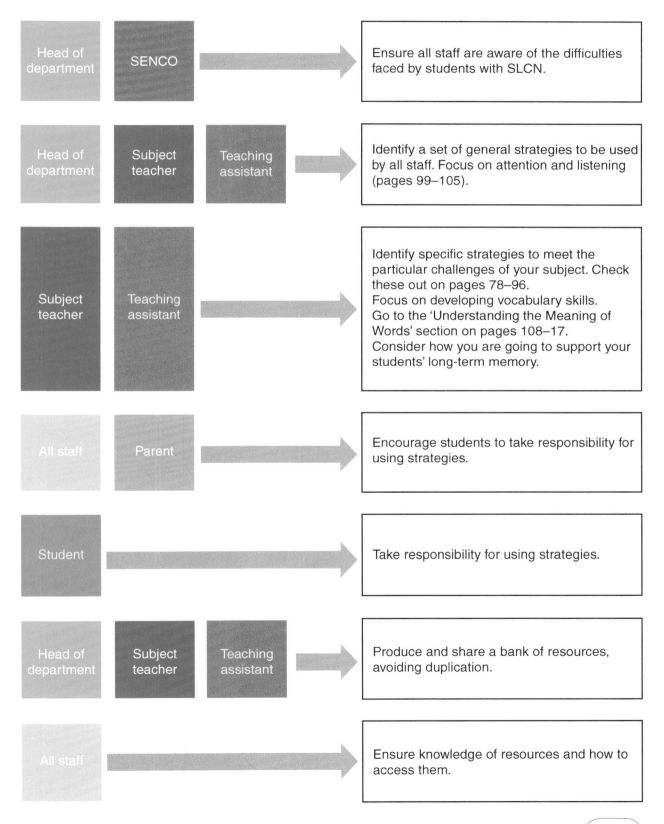

Head of department	SENCO	→	Ensure all staff are aware of the difficulties faced by students with SLCN.
Head of department	Subject teacher	Teaching assistant →	Identify a set of general strategies to be used by all staff. Focus on attention and listening (pages 99–105).
Subject teacher	Teaching assistant →		Identify specific strategies to meet the particular challenges of your subject. Check these out on pages 78–96. Focus on developing vocabulary skills. Go to the 'Understanding the Meaning of Words' section on pages 108–17. Consider how you are going to support your students' long-term memory.
All staff	Parent →		Encourage students to take responsibility for using strategies.
Student →			Take responsibility for using strategies.
Head of department	Subject teacher	Teaching assistant →	Produce and share a bank of resources, avoiding duplication.
All staff →			Ensure knowledge of resources and how to access them.

7 Record of Support

Name: Year:

NEED	STRATEGY	ADAPTATIONS	PROGRESSION
	Date:	Date:	Date:
	Date:	Date:	Date:
	Date:	Date:	Date:

Record of Support Example

Name: Ben Jones		Year: 7	
NEED	**STRATEGY**	**ADAPTATIONS**	**PROGRESSION**
Poor attention and listening in whole-class situations	**Active listening** **Cue cards taught in class – large cards displayed on wall CT points to remind** Date: 15. 09. 10	Introduced strip card for desk for reinforcement Date: 13.12.10	Removed strip card; occasional reminder with flip book Date: 14. 03. 11
Poor vocabulary retention and difficulty using traditional dictionary	**Semantic Word Book** **Whole class** **Group work reinforcement** Date: 24. 09.10	No adaptations necessary Date: 12.10.10	Made separate files for science, geography and RE Date: 14. 01.11
	Date:	Date:	Date:

ART AND DESIGN

Opportunities and Challenges across the Curriculum

Your subject offers the following opportunities for language and communication development. Each opportunity is also a possible challenge. To understand this further, go to the list of observed behaviours at the beginning of each language area in Chapter 5 (see column 3)

Consider using the following strategies to support students in meeting these challenges.

Go to Chapter 5. Explore the language area and find the strategy number, then look at the commercial resource list.

OPPORTUNITIES AND CHALLENGES	STRATEGIES AND SOLUTIONS	LANGUAGE AREA	STRATEGY NUMBER
• Listening to and processing instructions. • Selecting the correct equipment – knowing what it is called. • Remembering the sequence of what to do and when.	Work on active listening. Use visual cues. Label storage spaces with pictures/symbols and names of equipment. Use task-management boards.		16 17 18 21
• Understanding new terminology. • Developing thinking from concrete to abstract.	Use the 'What is it?' board. Provide visual support. Provide semantic dictionaries and word files. Teach abstract concepts by linking to a range of related concrete concepts.	BIG GROSS GIGANTIC ENORMOUS HUGE TALL	20 13 14 15 26

ART AND DESIGN

23	24	5
30		
![two faces icon]	![lightbulb icon]	![thought cloud icon]
• Working with others on joint projects. • Accepting praise and taking criticism.	• Visualising the finished product from a description.	• Explaining/discussing ideas. • Making judgements on quality, value and meaning.
Be clear about who is doing what. Use social rules posters. Provide opportunities to attend social skills groups. Make comments specific and honest.	Show finished examples. Teach visualising skills.	Teach the core vocabulary to talk about the idea. Start with everyday products, comparing their quality, etc. Always have visual material to support discussion.

DESIGN AND TECHNOLOGY

Your subject offers the following opportunities for language and communication development. Each opportunity is also a possible challenge. To understand this further, go to the list of observed behaviours at the beginning of each language area in Chapter 5 (see column 3)

Consider using the following strategies to support students in meeting these challenges.

Go to Chapter 5. Explore the language area and find the strategy number, then look at the commercial resource list.

OPPORTUNITIES AND CHALLENGES	STRATEGIES AND SOLUTIONS	LANGUAGE AREA	STRATEGY NUMBERS
Remembering the sequence of what to do when.	Use task-management boards.		21
New terminology.	Use the 'What is it?' board. Provide subject-specific semantic dictionaries and word files.		20 15 16
Working on joint projects. Accepting praise and taking criticism.	Be clear about roles. Use social rules posters. Encourage students to join social skills groups. Make sure comments are specific and honest.		23 30
Visualising the finished product from a description.	Show a finished example. Teach visualising skills.		24
Analysing existing products in order to inform new design.	Teach the core vocabulary to talk about the design of the product. Use symbols to represent elements. Provide a recording form divided into key elements for analysis.		5 7

ENGLISH

OPPORTUNITIES AND CHALLENGES	STRATEGIES AND SOLUTIONS	LANGUAGE AREA	STRATEGY NUMBERS
Your subject offers the following opportunities for language and communication development. Each opportunity is also a possible challenge. To understand this further, go to the list of observed behaviours at the beginning of each language area in Chapter 5 (see column 3)	Consider using the following strategies to support students in meeting these challenges.		Go to Chapter 5. Explore the language area and find the strategy number, then look at the commercial resource list.
• Listening to and processing instructions and information.	Work on active listening. Use visual cues. Use task-management boards and lesson schedules.		16 17 18 20 21
• Understanding the meaning of words and how they change in different contexts. • Understanding comprehension exercises. • Learning words with multiple meanings. • Remembering/understanding the plot and the relationships between characters in stories. • Generalising words/information.	Plan vocabulary and teach in a structured way. Use the 'What is it?' board. Provide semantic dictionaries and word files. Use colour-coding. Use word webs. Use mind maps and diagrams to illustrate the plot and how characters are related. Work with other departments on vocabulary development by practising its use across the curriculum within the same time frame.		6 7 20 15 16 17 13 13 6 7 10

ENGLISH

OPPORTUNITIES AND CHALLENGES	STRATEGIES AND SOLUTIONS	LANGUAGE AREA	STRATEGY NUMBERS
• Developing complex sentence structure.	Repeat using a simplified form.		4
	Use hand gestures for teaching tenses.		6
	Use resources such as BROGY.		Resource
	Teach grammatical structures – use written exercises.		8
			13
	Reinforce grammar through learning and reciting poetry/prose in groups.		7
• Understanding non-literal phrases.	Always explain. Use commercial resources.		12
• Putting oneself in another's place and empathising with characters from different periods of history, class or culture.	Relate to real-life experiences.		
	Role-play situations with student practising in more than one role.		
• Working on joint projects.	Be clear about who is doing what – give students with SLCN roles that will be successful.		23
	Use social rules posters.		30
	Provide opportunities to attend social skills groups.		31
• Using appropriate forms of communication for different situations.	Use role-play.		33

ENGLISH

• Visualising characters/scenes/situations from a description or in order to write a description.	Show pictures to accompany prose or to stimulate the imagination for creative writing. Teach visualising skills.	24
• Remembering and processing what has been said then formulating a related idea and remembering it until there is a chance to speak.	Use the ten-second rule and small discussion groups.	4
• Explaining/discussing ideas.	Teach the core vocabulary to talk about ideas. Use mind mapping.	8
• Selecting salient points.	Highlight text (comprehension exercises). Sort key points onto an 'order of importance' chart.	9
• Predicting outcomes.	Work on cause and effect.	13
• Organising information/thoughts.	Teach the core vocabulary. Provide discussion/writing frames.	
• Linking ideas and making connections.	Use mind mapping and flow charts.	8

HUMANITIES

Your subject offers the following opportunities for language and communication development. Each opportunity is also a possible challenge. To understand this further, go to the list of observed behaviours at the beginning of each language area in Chapter 5 (see column 3)

Consider using the following strategies to support students in meeting these challenges.

Go to Chapter 5. Explore the language area and find the strategy number, then look at the commercial resource list.

OPPORTUNITIES AND CHALLENGES	STRATEGIES AND SOLUTIONS	LANGUAGE AREA	STRATEGY NUMBERS
• Listening to and processing instructions. • Processing a high volume of new information. • Processing a large amount of auditory input.	Work on active listening. Use visual cues. Keep language simple. Chunk information. Include reinforcement activities in your delivery.	(ear image)	16 17 18 3 20
• Learning new vocabulary. • Generalising words/information. • Coping with concepts outside personal experience.	Pre-teach vocabulary. Provide semantic dictionaries and word files. Work with other departments on vocabulary development by practising its use across the curriculum within the same time frame. Visit relevant places to experience some aspects first-hand (a quarry/mine) or to set the scene (a castle/an air raid shelter) then record as a poster, diagram or flow chart. Watch DVDs.	BIG GROSS GIGANTIC ENORMOUS HUGE TALL	12 15 6 7 10 11 13

HUMANITIES

Skills	Strategies	Page
Having the ability to understand that others may have a different view of life.	Relate to real-life experiences.	30
	Role-play situations with the student practising in more than one role to experience other points of view.	31
Taking part in discussions and considering everyone's contribution by sharing focus of attention across a group.	Consider the dynamics of the group.	32
	Prompt listening to a number of different speakers.	33
	Be clear about roles.	
Working with others on joint projects.	Use social rules posters.	23
	Encourage students to join social skills groups.	30
Remembering instruction/information long enough to process and reply to it.	Use the ten-second rule.	4
Remembering the point you want to make while waiting for a turn in the conversation.	Note taking.	
Explaining/discussing ideas and aims.	Teach the core vocabulary.	5
Ability to extract and organise relevant information.	Use questioning strategies.	3
Comparing different ways of life and points of view.	Use mind mapping followed by sequencing main points from the mind maps.	8
Weighing up advantages and disadvantages.		4
Considering causes of change.		9
Distinguishing between facts and opinion.		11
Comparing interpretations of an event.		

MATHS

OPPORTUNITIES AND CHALLENGES	STRATEGIES AND SOLUTIONS	LANGUAGE AREA	STRATEGY NUMBERS
Your subject offers the following opportunities for language and communication development. Each opportunity is also a possible challenge. To understand this further, go to the list of observed behaviours at the beginning of each language area in Chapter 5 (see column 3)	Consider using the following strategies to support students in meeting these challenges.		Go to Chapter 5. Explore the language area and find the strategy number, then look at the commercial resource list.
Listening to and processing instructions.	Work on active listening. Use visual cues. Always make the order of action the order of mention.		16 17 13
Selecting equipment and calling it by the correct name.	Label storage spaces with pictures/symbols and names of equipment.		
Learning the order in which to do tasks within a maths activity.	Use task-management boards.		21
Discriminating between similar-sounding numbers, e.g. sixty and sixteen.	When talking about numbers, speak clearly, writing any that could be misheard on the white board as you speak.		

MATHS

Area	Strategy	Ref
Learning the basics – days of the week, months of the year, quantity, volume, tables, etc.	Do not assume retained knowledge of this. Refer regularly to information pasted on to maths book/file or displayed on wall.	
Understanding time concepts.	Visual timetables. See p. 101 (19).	18
	Use personal time line – days of the week blocks.	
Understanding prepositions.	Use hand positioning.	20
Understanding question words.	These are often confusing for students with SLCN. Use question cue cards with symbols. See p. 133 (3)	27
Using words that have different meanings in other contexts, i.e. table, form, value, figure.	Explain when using the word.	13
	Use word web posters.	14
	Consider using recording devices to provide students with talking glossaries/instruction cards.	
Collecting data.	Practise asking questions and recording through role-play (including how to greet and round-off).	31
	Provide clear simple sheets for collecting information.	
Working in a group on a joint project.	Be clear about who is doing what.	
	Use social rules posters.	23
	Provide opportunities to attend social skills groups.	30

Icons: BIG GROSS GIGANTIC ENORMOUS HUGE TALL

MATHS

OPPORTUNITIES AND CHALLENGES	STRATEGIES AND SOLUTIONS	LANGUAGE AREA	STRATEGY NUMBERS
• Retaining information long enough to work out what it all means and work out the maths. • Retaining information, selecting the appropriate method and working out maths internally.	Use task management boards. Allow students to use external recording methods to increase confidence. Consider using raps, rhymes and songs to reinforce information – very powerful memory jogger.		14 7 23
• Extracting relevant information. • Developing sequencing skills. • Explaining a process/method. • Linking ideas and making connections. • Developing flexibility of thinking as maths requires students to use a range of skills – switching from one to another during the same activity.	Use colour-coding. Use question cue cards. Provide recording frameworks suitable for the task, e.g. flow charts for sequencing and explaining a process or method, mind maps and Venn diagrams for connecting ideas. List key words to prompt which skill to use. Teach the rules and point out the logic.		9 3 12

MFL

Go to Chapter 5. Explore the language area and find the strategy number, then look at the commercial resource list.

Your subject offers the following opportunities for language and communication development. Each opportunity is also a possible challenge. To understand this further, go to the list of observed behaviours at the beginning of each language area in Chapter 5 (see column 3)

Consider using the following strategies to support students in meeting these challenges.

OPPORTUNITIES AND CHALLENGES	STRATEGIES AND SOLUTIONS	LANGUAGE AREA	STRATEGY NUMBERS
• Listening to and retaining unfamiliar sounds, words and phrases.	Use recording devices for students to practise sounds/words and to listen to the correct form.		30 31
• Learning new words for vocabulary that is already understood. • Pace may be an issue – new vocabulary introduced too quickly to assimilate.	Reduce the number of words to learn. Encourage role-play in small groups. Provide visual support. Use sales catalogues and flyers in new language for cutting out and sorting.		25
• Learning a new grammatical structure and rule system. • Flexibility in applying grammatical rules.	Using visual sentence planners.		7 18 13
• Working on everyday topics – good opportunity to practise social skills and revisit situations not fully understood.	Work in small groups/pairs to use ideas from social skills group activities. Role-play situations.		30 31
• Using unfamiliar speech patterns – repetitious practice at producing unfamiliar sounds and words within a group having the same experience.	Practise sounds as a whole class or in small groups.		

89

MUSIC

OPPORTUNITIES AND CHALLENGES	STRATEGIES AND SOLUTIONS	LANGUAGE AREA	STRATEGY NUMBERS
Your subject offers the following opportunities for language and communication development. Each opportunity is also a possible challenge. To understand this further, go to the list of observed behaviours at the beginning of each language area in Chapter 5 (see column 3)	Consider using the following strategies to support students in meeting these challenges.	Go to Chapter 5. Explore the language area and find the strategy number, then look at the commercial resource list.	
• Listening and attending. • Auditory discrimination. • Remembering the sequence of what to do when.	Work on active listening. Play sound bingo using everyday sounds, moving on to musical instruments. Use task-management boards.		17 18 21
• Understanding new terminology.	Use subject-specific word books/files. Recording devices as a talking glossary.	BIG GROSS GIGANTIC ENORMOUS HUGE TALL	15 14
• Low on language demands. • Development of many skills underpinning communication and literacy, e.g. aural perception, rhyming, oral discrimination, patterns of spoken language, etc.	Take this opportunity to set language to music/raps and chants to help students expand on sentence structure and narrative skills.		

MUSIC

No.	Strategy	Skill
23	Take this opportunity to set language to music/raps and chants to help students remember salient points from other subjects.	• Can be used to support memory, e.g. using chanting and songs to learn words, phrases and factual information.
12	Work on 'same and different'. Start with the sounds musical instruments make – use a Venn diagram to record.	• An ability to compare pieces of music.
11	Use sorting and classifying activities.	• An understanding of different genres and the influences that have created them.
25	Use cue cards with pictures/symbols representing each emotion. Make sure students have the language to talk about emotion.	• The ability to talk about music in relation to emotion.

PHYSICAL EDUCATION

OPPORTUNITIES AND CHALLENGES *Your subject offers the following opportunities for language and communication development. Each opportunity is also a possible challenge. To understand this further, go to the list of observed behaviours at the beginning of each language area in chapter 5 (see column 3)*	STRATEGIES AND SOLUTIONS *Consider using the following strategies to support students in meeting these challenges.*	LANGUAGE AREA	STRATEGY NUMBERS *Go to Chapter 5. Explore the language area and find the strategy number, then look at the commercial resource list.*
• Understanding rules in games from verbal instructions.	Pre-teach rules using diagrams and role-playing parts of the game. Use visual cue cards as reminders.		16 17 18
• Selecting the correct equipment – knowing what it is called.	Label equipment and the place where it is stored. Provide word web posters showing which sports equipment is required for which game.	BIG GROSS GIGANTIC ENORMOUS HUGE TALL	13

PHYSICAL EDUCATION

	Numbers	Strategy	Issues
	2 6 15 17	You may need to spend more time helping students with SLCN to understand safety requirements in PE. Do not give too much explanation – use symbols and clear, simple instructions. Learn by rote. Give very clear directions. Make sure all rules are understood. Keep students focused – use cue cards.	• Safety issues. • Getting ready for PE – coping in the changing rooms. • Working with others as a team and in opposition.
	4 12	Provide task-management boards or flow diagrams in poster form. Use mnemonics.	• Remembering the sequence of what to do when.
	12	Provide an ideas frame and a flow chart frame. Be clear about roles.	• Working with others to create a gym or dance sequence.

PSHE

OPPORTUNITIES AND CHALLENGES	STRATEGIES AND SOLUTIONS	LANGUAGE AREA	STRATEGY NUMBERS
• Developing an understanding of the language to talk about personal identity, healthy lifestyles, risk, relationships and diversity.	Provide semantic dictionaries and word files. Work with other departments on vocabulary development by practising its use across the curriculum within the same time frame.	BIG GROSS GIGANTIC ENORMOUS HUGE TALL	15
• Learning words to discuss emotion. • Opportunities to discuss issues for students with SLCN. • Discussion about relationships, their importance and how everyone has to learn how to relate well with others and practise these skills. • Emotional issues can be aired.	Work specifically on words to do with emotion using cue cards and role-play. Consider contributing towards the 'Language-Friendly School' initiative in project work. Choose groups carefully – do not include more than one student with SLCN in the same group and if possible provide adult support. Work with staff who are running a social communication skills group so that topic/skills training is related to PSHE lessons.		25 17 18 23 30 31 33

Go to Chapter 5. Explore the language area and find the strategy number, then look at the commercial resource list.

Consider using the following strategies to support students in meeting these challenges.

Your subject offers the following opportunities for language and communication development. Each opportunity is also a possible challenge. To understand this further, go to the list of observed behaviours at the beginning of each language area in Chapter 5 (see column 3)

SCIENCE

Your subject offers the following opportunities for language and communication development. Each opportunity is also a possible challenge. To understand this further, go to the list of observed behaviours at the beginning of each language area in Chapter 5 (see column 3)

Consider using the following strategies to support students in meeting these challenges.

Go to Chapter 5. Explore the language area and find the strategy number, then look at the commercial resource list.

OPPORTUNITIES AND CHALLENGES	STRATEGIES AND SOLUTIONS	LANGUAGE AREA	STRATEGY NUMBERS
• Selecting the correct equipment and knowing what it is called. • Sequencing processes. • Remembering the sequence of what to do when. • Processing a high volume of new information.	Label storage spaces with pictures/symbols and names of equipment. Use task-management boards. Use visual cues. Keep language simple and chunk information. Refer to posters, diagrams on the classroom wall.		21 3 16 17 18
• Learning new vocabulary.	Pre-teach vocabulary. Provide semantic dictionaries and word files. Teach simple word definitions. Use recording devices to produce talking glossaries. Provide fun activities to reinforce vocabulary.	BIG GROSS GIGANTIC ENORMOUS HUGE TALL	12 15 20 14

SCIENCE

OPPORTUNITIES AND CHALLENGES	STRATEGIES AND SOLUTIONS	LANGUAGE AREA	STRATEGY NUMBERS
• Safety issues.	You may need to spend more time helping students with SLCN to understand safety requirements in science. Do not give too much explanation – use symbols and clear, simple instructions. Learn by rote.		2 6 8
• Working on joint projects.	Make sure the group has at least one student with good language skills. Give clear directions, making sure that the student with SLCN can make a successful contribution. Use a group rules poster.		23
• Remembering instruction/information long enough to process and reply to it.	Use the tensecond rule.		4 12
• Teaching in science is visual and hands on, which makes it easier to understand and therefore remember.	Add mnemonics and mind mapping.		11
• Organising information/thoughts.	Teach the core vocabulary. Provide structured recording sheets.		5 6
• Linking ideas and making connections.	Use mind mapping followed by sequencing the main points from the mind maps.		7
• Selecting salient points.	Sort key points onto an 'order of importance' chart.		8
• Predicting outcomes.	Work on cause and effect in everyday situations and use as analogies.		13
• Solving problems, arriving at conclusions, etc.	Develop the ability to ask questions. Use question cue cards.		3

5 Strategies for Use across the Curriculum

This chapter aims to provide practitioners with a wealth of strategy and activity ideas to support students with language and communication needs across all areas of the curriculum. It is divided into the six areas of language identified in Chapter 2. Each area is colour- and symbol-coded to match the Language for Learning model of speech, language and communication skills and lists typical behaviours observed in students who have difficulties in that area. It also provides practitioners with a range of strategy and activity ideas to support students across the curriculum. The suggestions are a starting point and will need to be adapted to be national curriculum-friendly and suited to the needs of individual students and settings.

The strategy ideas are sub-divided into:

- *positive communication* – ways practitioners can improve their delivery;

- *universal strategies and approaches* – inclusive practice for the benefit of all young people;

- *targeted strategies and approaches* – support for those students identified as having SLCN.

Finally, there are examples of how these strategies can be presented to parents so development can continue at home. Resources are suggested and their sources named. More information on these sources can be found in the Appendix.

Introducing Strategies and Resources

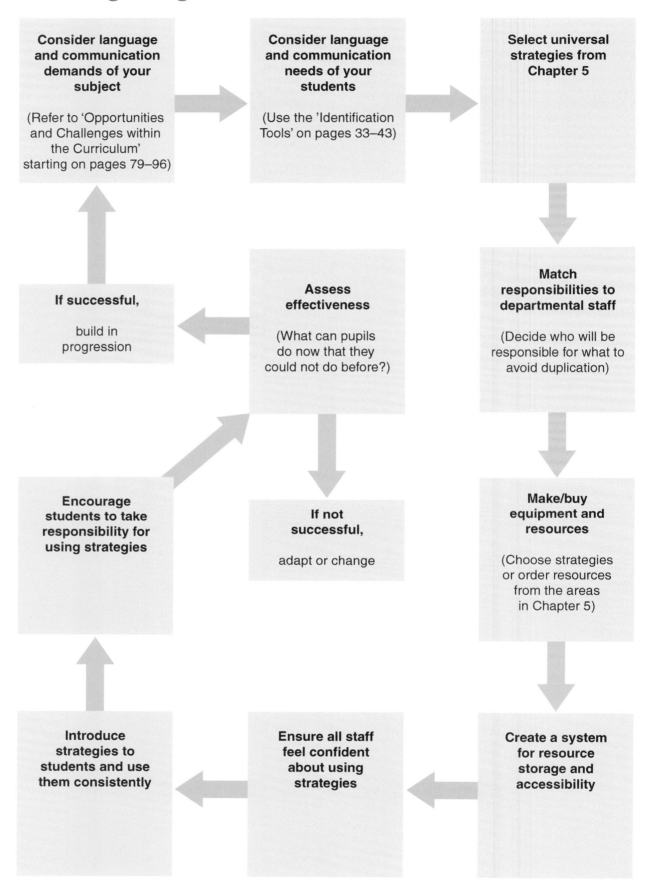

Consider language and communication demands of your subject

(Refer to 'Opportunities and Challenges within the Curriculum' starting on pages 79–96)

Consider language and communication needs of your students

(Use the 'Identification Tools' on pages 33–43)

Select universal strategies from Chapter 5

Match responsibilities to departmental staff

(Decide who will be responsible for what to avoid duplication)

If successful,

build in progression

Assess effectiveness

(What can pupils do now that they could not do before?)

Encourage students to take responsibility for using strategies

If not successful,

adapt or change

Make/buy equipment and resources

(Choose strategies or order resources from the areas in Chapter 5)

Introduce strategies to students and use them consistently

Ensure all staff feel confident about using strategies

Create a system for resource storage and accessibility

Attention and Listening

Observed Behaviours

- Fails to attend to the speaker.
- Experiences difficulties sustaining attention and listening skills across a variety of contexts.
- Lacks motivation to listen – those students who are aware that processing auditory information is demanding may 'switch off' or lack motivation to engage in verbal discussions.
- Is more able to engage when visual or kinaesthetic learning opportunities are presented.
- Experiences difficulties integrating attention, e.g. processing both the auditory and visual information.
- Is distracted by redundant information, e.g. extraneous noise.
- Experiences fatigue following activities that require sustained listening.
- Day dreams.

Positive Ways to Communicate

1 Speak clearly – give clear short instructions and chunk information. If you have an accent, be aware of regional terms you may use and how your phrasing may appear odd to your students. The larger the class, the slower you need to speak.

2 Secure attention by saying the student's name.

3 Keep language simple – pitch vocabulary and grammar at a level that the class can understand.

4 Identify new vocabulary and explain it – remember that students have had different levels of exposure to vocabulary. Terms not in everyday use need to be explained.

5 Re-word key sentences – complex sentences containing unfamiliar vocabulary may need to be re-worded.

6   Explain idioms and non-literal language as many students have difficulties understanding idioms such as 'I'm tearing my hair out' or non-literal language such as 'I want you to work so hard there'll be steam coming off the paper'. It is important to use this type of language as it is so much a part of our culture, but it must be explained.

7   Ask students to repeat back what they have to do. When students have repeated an instruction out loud they have more chance of remembering it.

8   Position students so that eye contact can be maintained. During discussion times arrange seating so that students can establish eye contact. Encourage students to look at the speaker when questions are asked in class, even if this means turning around.

9   Allow a variety of noise levels in class – vary your acceptance of noise level to meet the demands of different speaking and listening activities.

10   Alter seating so that concentration is maintained. Position students who are easily distracted near you. Use screens to make study booths.

11   Give the student time to process what has been said by using the ten-second rule – once you have given an instruction allow the student ten seconds to respond. During this time, consider the instruction: Were there too many words? Was the vocabulary too difficult to understand? If the student does not respond after ten seconds, either rephrase the instruction or, if the right level of language was used the first time, simply repeat the instruction again.

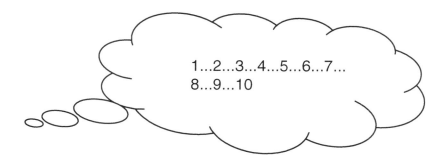

1...2...3...4...5...6...7...8...9...10

12   Use positive statements about what the student should do, e.g. 'Start your work' rather than 'Stop messing about'.

13 Give instructions in the same order as the action required, e.g. 'Finish the sentence you are writing, then get your homework books' rather than 'Get your homework books after you have finished the sentence you are writing.'

14 Encourage students to 'rehearse' what they have heard by saying it over and over silently. (This may have to be done out loud to begin with.)

15 Check understanding by asking open-ended questions after information has been given, e.g. 'Which book do you have to use?', 'How are you going to start?'

Universal Strategies and Approaches

16 Use visual cues, gesture and/or signing to accompany verbal instructions or information, e.g. have objects, pictures or diagrams and flow charts illustrating topic work handy to accompany new vocabulary or concepts.

17 Teach 'active listening' by showing students that in order to listen effectively they must sit still, look at the speaker and think about what is being said (Johnson and Player 2009). Use picture cue cards to support students' understanding of each skill, e.g. look, sit, think and listen.

18 Develop students' ability to take responsibility for not understanding by creating a culture in the classroom that gives them the confidence to say if they (a) couldn't hear, (b) didn't understand the words you used or (c) had difficulty with the pace. Do this by specifically teaching them how to do it and praising them when they do. 'Seeking clarification' cue cards are useful for this. See commercially available materials list.

19 Make timetables visual by adding symbols and colour-coding. Have large versions displayed on classroom walls so that they can be used to support the development of skills such as sequencing and recall and the understanding of specific time concepts, such as yesterday, last week, the day after tomorrow, etc.

20 Support listening and processing of new information by providing a 'comic strip' series of pictures illustrating the main points. For example, during the First World War, Lloyd George had three main tactics to ensure that people in Britain didn't starve. A card with a symbol/picture and a short sentence representing each tactic could be provided.

21 Support students' ability to listen to and understand instructions by using task-management boards which provide pictorial and/or written support of the stages within a single activity.

TASK-MANAGEMENT BOARD	
Task: Equipment:	
1.	
2.	
3.	
4.	
5.	
I will be finished when:	I can now:

22 Give students a verbal message to give to another member of staff or class. The message should require an answer so that it is clear that the instruction was delivered correctly.

23 Ask students to listen out for a specific fact/s before watching a DVD or listening to information and, when they hear it, to give a signal in some way – put their hands up, clap or make a note of what was actually said. For example, while learning about the carbon cycle ask students to listen out for the four ways carbon can find its way back into the air. Different information could be listened for by different pupils, so varying the level of difficulty can be used.

24 Start the lesson with a short focusing activity. For example, in maths count to 20 in 2s; in geography ask each student in turn to name a capital city, a river, etc., going through the letters of the alphabet. This will help students to switch focus to a new subject.

25 Use peer support through pair work – able student presents story or information to an audience while his/her partner (pupil with language difficulties) provides gesture/picture cue cards.

26 Have a separate board in form rooms for daily instructions. When giving out notices at registration times write in note form what you're saying on to a notice board kept for this purpose. Leave the notices all day so that students may pop back and re-read them. Before writing new ones, check that the previous ones have been acted upon. Use different colours for different types of notices, e.g. blue for things that have to be brought from home, green for changes in timetable, red for school trips, etc.

Targeted Strategies and Approaches

27 Seat students so they can all see each other. Ask each student in turn to tell the rest of the class something about themselves. When everyone has had a turn, ask questions like, 'What did Carl say?' or 'Who likes "heavy metal" music?' Adapt this for the plenary – after students have given their report ask the group questions about what has been said.

28 Play 'speaker, listener, observer'. The speaker tells the group about something, the listener re-tells the incident, then the observer comments on how much information the listener remembered. At first it is best if the speaker is an adult who keeps the 'narrative' simple and within the students' experience. Later, it is a useful group activity to reinforce information from current topic work.

29 Use photographs or symbols to develop the ability to process instructions. Select a group of pictures which belong together, e.g. cooking equipment and ingredients, then suggest a recipe. Say to the student, 'We are going to make.... You will need....' The students make their selection then you tell them the method, and the pictures are sequenced accordingly. Gradually increase the number you ask for and increase the difficulty of processing by including objects of, maybe, different colours and asking for a particular one. This strategy is easily adapted for use across the curriculum, e.g. 'Go to the sports hall and set out the following equipment: six hoops, six balls, six bean bags and six ropes.' Give the student(s) a photograph of how it should look, next time let them look at the photograph, but not take it with them and finally expect them to do it without a visual cue.

30 For students who have poor auditory discrimination, provide short 'ice-breaker' activities at the start of group work. Consider the following suggestions:

a Commercial auditory discrimination resources.

b Record familiar sounds or well-known voices from around the school and take photos for matching.

c Play 'Listen to the Silence' – sit very quietly whispering the names of the things that can be heard.

d Play an unfamiliar pop song, asking students what instruments they could hear or what lyrics they remembered.

e Play 'Join in Clap' – one person claps a simple rhythm and each pupil joins in, in turn, until everyone is clapping the same rhythm.

f Play 'Copy Clap' – as above, but each student claps in turn so that they practise remembering the rhythm.

31 Use recording devices for (a) vital information so that students can listen repeatedly or (b) for students to record their ideas so they will not be forgotten.

32 Play barrier games – put a screen between two students and introduce activities which require giving and receiving instructions. Use worksheets that contain pictures of current topic vocabulary – a diagram of a plant, the characters in a novel or the instruments in an orchestra, for example. Each student has the same worksheet and an identical set of coloured pencils. The students take it in turn to give an instruction such as, 'Colour the stamen red' or 'Circle the largest wind instrument in blue', etc. Both students then carry out all of the instructions and the sheets are compared at the end. To start with it may be necessary to do this with an adult giving the instruction to a group of students.

Commercially Available Material

- 'Active listening' cue cards – Language for Learning
- 'Seeking clarification' cue cards – Language for Learning
- Task-management boards – Language for Learning
- 'Tune into...' series – Yellow Door
- Active Listening for Active Learning – QED
- 'Good listening' and 'Good talking' posters – TaskMaster
- Communicate in Print – Widgit Software
- Visual Timetable Software – Surer Steps
- TrackMaker Plus – Surer Steps
- Visual Planner – Surer Steps
- IEPicture Maker – Surer Steps
- Mystifying Metaphors and Smiley Similes – Bird Art
- Don't Take It So Literally – Winslow
- What Did You Say? What Did You Mean? – Jessica Kingsley

Using Strategies at Home

STRATEGY	PARENTS	STUDENT	COMMENTS Make notes to improve/adapt the strategy – discuss with the SENCO or TA
Visual Timetable This will help to understand/develop: 1. what will happen next/during the day; 2. what expectations there are; 3. abstract concepts related to time, e.g. first, second, third, last, next, today, tomorrow, yesterday, days of the week, date, etc.; 4. general communication skills, i.e. attention skills, listening, commenting, questioning, discussing past and future events, recall and prediction; 5. general organisational skills, i.e. top–bottom working and left–right working; 6. independent working.	This timetable (with instructions) will be provided by school. Try to use it daily with your child. Provide similar timetables for activities/events at home, i.e. evening activities, school holidays, etc.	Use your visual timetable so that you are ready for school. It will help you to have the right equipment for the right day, to get homework in on time, to ask questions about lessons/activities in advance so that you feel more confident and talk to your parents/friends about what has been interesting and what you like/don't like. It will also help you to learn a lot of new words and the names of your teachers and helpers.	

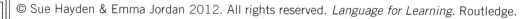

STRATEGY	PARENTS	STUDENT	COMMENTS Make notes to improve/adapt the strategy – discuss with the SENCO or TA
Task-management Boards These work like a recipe, helping to complete tasks by listing equipment and the order in which to do things. They work because they: 1. have less language to process; 2. reduce the load on memory; 3. develop organisational skills; 4. support independent working.	An example will be given to you by school. Your child may bring task-management boards home to help with homework. You can make them to help your child do things independently at home. Go through the strip to make sure that each step and the final result is understood. Help him/her to move along from one stage to the next by referring to the strip. Move on to preparing the strip together, asking him/her to guess what will be next on the strip. Once this has become familiar, encourage him/her to use the strip independently.	Use task-management boards so that your home work and jobs at home are easier to do. They will help you to get the right equipment, know exactly what you have to do and what to do first, second, third and so on.	
Home–School Link Book This will help to: 1. remember and sequence factual information; 2. report on events which have taken place; 3. interpret social situations; 4. make sense of new experiences and remember the 'how', 'what' and 'when', etc., of homework.	This will be provided by school. A teacher or TA will write about things to do with school and you can write about things to do with home so that it is easy to chat. The sort of things you will write about are: 1. information about future events, topics and news (e.g. 'we went to Alton Towers at the weekend and…'). Give a quick summary of something that your child enjoyed/didn't enjoy; 2. a social or behavioural situation that may have been confusing to your child; 3. a new experience that he/she had to deal with. Your child should see this book as a 'friend' so it is important that it is kept as neutral as possible and not used as a way of reporting on his/her behaviour, his/her inability to cope or the problems you are having.	A home–school link book will make it easy for you to talk to your parents and teachers about things going on in your life. Your teachers and parents will not write anything that you do not want to talk about or you do not want everyone to know. Tell them what you would like to include and listen to their suggestions. You might like to attach things like brochures, tickets or photos.	

Understanding the Meaning of Words

Observed Behaviours

- Having limited or weak vocabulary skills with gaps in everyday vocabulary.

- Saying 'I've heard that word before', such as in relation to subject-specific vocabulary, but not being able to demonstrate any understanding of the meaning of a word.

- Using or reading language without understanding its meaning, e.g. using sophisticated vocabulary but then when questioned being unable to say what the word means.

- Experiencing difficulties learning, retaining and then retrieving subject-based vocabulary.

- Learning a word in one situation but then experiencing difficulties applying it or generalising its use.

- Experiencing difficulties defining words, including identifying similarities or differences between word meanings.

- Experiencing greater difficulty with more abstract concepts, e.g. time concepts – 'next week', 'last term', 'the day after tomorrow'.

- Being inflexible with vocabulary, e.g. becoming confused with words with multiple meanings.

- Struggling to find the right word – hesitating, using a similar word, using gesture or mime to compensate or creating new words.

Positive Communication

1 Reinforce vocabulary by giving students experience of target words in as many different contexts and with as many different adults as possible. Link new vocabulary to concrete objects, use in role-play situations and illustrate with pictures/symbols.

2 Reduce anxiety by not insisting on the correct word; be accepting of a description or a similar word, but use the correct word in your reply, e.g. 'It's the thing that has a bow and you hold it on your shoulder – the small one.' 'Yes, that's right; it's the violin.'

3 Some students may find it helpful if you cue them in first, with the initial sound, then the first syllable, then second syllable, etc. For example, 'ph … pho … photo … photosyn….', etc. However, others may find this a distraction.

4 Some students need time to recall the appropriate word – it may be helpful to move on to the next question with another student, asking the first student to let you know when they have remembered.

5 Use the visual materials that support subject vocabulary displayed on classroom walls by referring to them as you speak – students need reminding that they are there.

Universal Strategies and Approaches

6 Adopt a systematic approach to teaching new vocabulary – choose both concrete and abstract concepts related to topic vocabulary and prioritise the vocabulary for students to understand/use.

7 Reinforce the meaning of the word, not just the label/name. For example, 'It's an estuary, you find it where a river goes into the sea.'

8 Check understanding by asking open-ended questions after information has been given, e.g. 'What do you know about liquid iron?'.

9 Develop an awareness of 'same' and 'different' to support understanding of similarities and differences. Identify the differences between words to help students develop new word concepts by sorting and categorising.

10 Teach new vocabulary in meaningful learning situations, using real objects and tapping into visual, auditory and kinaesthetic learning styles.

11 Do not assume that students will generalise the use of vocabulary from one context to another – provide visual clues to help students to do this.

12 Provide pre-teaching opportunities. Use topic books/revision guides for a lower Key Stage so that information can be 'scaffolded' from simple to more difficult.

13 Use visual materials to support the understanding of links between words, concepts and processes, for example:

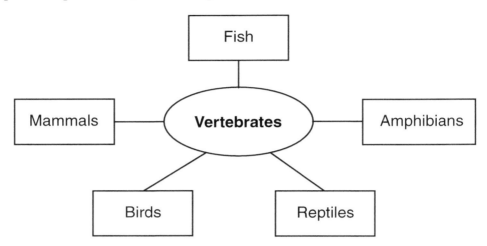

Word webs help to show the relationship between words or those that have multiple meanings. Mind maps, developed by Tony Buzan, see p. 141, provide visual semantic links between words. Arrange topic displays as a mind map on classroom walls. Provide simple mind maps of each curriculum topic and teach students to record their own work in mind map form. Use mind mapping to gather information about what students know before introducing a new topic. Mind map again once the topic is completed and compare the difference with students to illustrate how much they have learned.

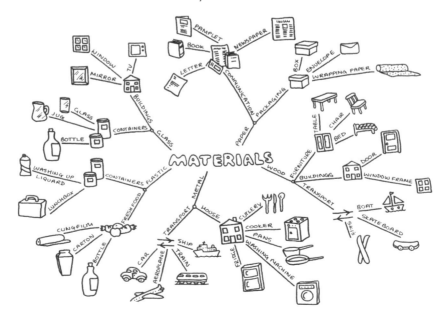

Flow diagrams support sequencing skills so are useful to explain a process.

14 Use recording devices as talking glossaries.

15 Use personal word books or files organised by category. When students request a spelling, rather than asking for the initial sound, ask them to find the category that the word belongs to. The word is then recorded with related words which helps students to both understand the meaning of the word and also store it more effectively in his/her long-term memory. Choose about 20 categories to begin with and provide both the picture and the word. Stick these throughout the word book/file to create sections. Gradually increase the complexity by further dividing into sub-categories to increase the level of semantic understanding. Consider using this method within subject areas.

16 Use commercial visual dictionaries to support understanding rather than traditional dictionaries that use language to describe language.

17 Use colour and icons to help organise language. Decide on a colour-code for your subject. For example, in science all things to do with heat could be red, everything to do with growth green. In maths, colour all words to do with addition red, subtraction yellow, multiplication blue, etc. Put symbols by instructions to help students decide what has to be done, e.g. an 'open book' by the part that has to be read, a 'pen' by the part that has to be written, a 'light bulb' when the student's own ideas are required, etc.

18 Place a visual timeline around the form room with the main school events marked. Include holidays, assignment dates, special activities and social events. Attach a moveable arrow pinpointing the current day. Refer to it regularly, discussing time management.

Targeted Strategies and Approaches

19 Play barrier games – put a screen between two students and introduce activities which require giving and receiving instructions. Use worksheets that contain pictures of current topic vocabulary – a diagram of a plant, the characters in a novel or the instruments in an orchestra, for example.

Each student has the same worksheet and an identical set of coloured pencils. The students take it in turns to give an instruction such as, 'Colour the stamen red' or 'Circle the largest wind instrument in blue', etc. Both students then carry out all of the instructions and the sheets are compared at the end. To start with it may be necessary to do this with an adult giving the instruction to a group of students.

20 Develop word definition skills by asking questions related to the meaning of a word. For instance, 'What do you do with it?', 'Where do you find it?', 'What sound does it begin with?', 'How many syllables does it have?', 'What does it rhyme with?', 'What does it look/smell/taste like?'. The 'What is it?' board and 'Word definition' cue cards (see commercial resources) are useful for this.

21 Place a collection of objects, pictures or words from current topic work in front of a small group of students. Describe one of the objects, asking the students to guess what it is. Gradually involve students as the describers.

22 Play versions of 'I went to the market and I bought…' depending on the subject vocabulary you want to teach. For example, the first student might say: 'I'm going to make a tie-dyed scarf so I will need some cotton material.' The second student responds, 'I'm going to make a tie-dyed scarf so I will need some cotton material and some bees' wax.' This can be extended to add a reason why the product is needed.

23 Play 'snap' and 'pelmanism', matching words and word definitions with pictures.

24 Play 'I spy', targeting topic vocabulary and using a description rather than a letter name, e.g. 'I spy with my little eye something that is brown, square, has a shoulder strap and contains something to help me breathe during an air raid.'

25 Sorting and classifying, often neglected in the secondary school, is a very useful strategy to support students' understanding and memory of new vocabulary. Use as many objects, pictures and ways of sorting as possible. Start with just two classifications, e.g. 'gas and not gas'/'liquid and not liquid'/'solids and not solids', then increase to 'gas and liquid', then to 'gas, liquid and solids'.

26 Using vocabulary from current topic work, learn the abstract words by linking them to known concrete words. For example, lay out large pictures representing 'the Houses of Parliament', 'a politician', 'a computer' and a 'pot plant'. Place the following words onto cards and attach them to one or more of the pictures: solid, old, happy, beautiful, healthy, tall, delicate, hungry, grand, latest, heavy, nervous, shiny.

27 Once students understand the function and location of objects, teach them how to describe. To begin with, practise using two elements only – size and colour. For example, 'It's big and blue.' Gradually add words linked to the senses: 'What does it look like?', 'What does it feel like?', 'What does it sound like?', 'Does it have a taste?', 'Does it have a smell?'. The 'Word association' cue cards (see commercial resources) are useful for this.

28 Using cue cards as described above, give one to each student then pass an object around. As each student receives the object he/she thinks of a word to describe it from the cue card they have. For example, if the object is a magnet, the first student has the 'colour' cue card and her response is 'Silvery grey with red tips'; the next student has the 'size' card and says 'Small and chunky'. Gradually increase expectation so the cue card word and the description is included and the student is repeating what has been said before; for example, 'The magnet is silvery grey with red tips and is small and chunky'.

29 Pass a picture or object related to current topic work around the group. As each student receives it they (a) add a word to describe it, (b) explain what it could be used for and (c) offer something that it is associated with.

30 Students take it in turns to describe a person, object or place from their current topic for the rest of the group to guess. The 'describer' is given a picture of the person/object/place and a cue card listing a range of associations to help with the description (function, location, parts, category, starts with…, rhymes with…, has … syllables…, sounds like…, smells like…, shape, colour, size, etc.).

31 Provide picture and word boards to support topic vocabulary for groups to refer to while listening to information, completing work in class or at home.

Commercially Available Material

- 'Word association' cue cards – Language for Learning
- 'What is it?' boards and posters – Language for Learning
- Maths concept wheel – Language for Learning
- Photo cards – LDA
- Colour cards – Winslow
- Bringing Words to Life – The Guilford Press
- Combimage – Winslow
- The If Game – Philip & Tacey
- Homonyms/Synonyms – Smartkids
- How to be Brilliant at... series – Brilliant Publications
- Kidspiration and Inspiration – Semerc
- Mind Maps for Kids – Thorsons
- Mind Maps for Kids: Rev up for Revision – Thorsons
- The Mind Map Book: Radiant Thinking – BBC Books
- Revision guides – Co-ordination Group Publications (CGP); Letts Education; Collins

Using Strategies at Home

STRATEGY	PARENTS	STUDENT	COMMENTS Make notes to improve/adapt the strategy – discuss with the SENCO or TA
'What Is It?' Poster The 'What is it?' poster is a way of teaching your child new words. Words are best taught in a systematic way and revised frequently. This poster helps to do this by linking the word to its associations.	Your school will provide you with a copy of the poster, the words your child is learning at the moment, a picture to represent each word and a sentence or two to say what it means. This is what you do: 1. Say the word. 2. Look at the picture of the word and place it in the centre of the 'What is it?' poster. 3. Work around the board, discussing each section. Function (What does it do? What is it used for?) Location (Where do we find it? Where does it live?) What parts does it have? What category does it belong to?). Ask your child to clap out the syllables of the word, to think of some rhyming words (these can be real or nonsense words) followed by the sound the word starts with. Continue by thinking about its attributes – smell, taste, colour, shape, etc., and finally what feelings you have about it. 4. Think about the meaning of the word and help your child to say what the word means; talk about different situations the word is used in and then put the word into a sentence. 5. Put the picture and word up in your child's bedroom or on the fridge and revise it regularly.	This is a fun way to learn new words – it will help your parents too because they will not know all of them. There may be words you hear to do with out-of-school activities – get an adult to write them down and practise learning them this way too.	

115

STRATEGY	PARENTS	STUDENT	COMMENTS Make notes to improve/adapt the strategy – discuss with the SENCO or TA
Mind Mapping Mind mapping is useful as it reduces language load to single key words, each representing an element of the concept being learned. A mind map is an efficient memory jogger; the key words are readily expanded into sentences and the sentences into paragraphs. So, in summary, mind mapping supports our language skills in a number of ways by: 1. recording information logically and linking it to what is already known; 2. grouping vocabulary in a way that helps to understand it, store it in our long-term memory and remember it when we need it; 3. helping to think of sentences and a plot when using it for story writing; 4. helping to remember information in more depth for assignments and exams; 5. helping presentation skills during assemblies and assessments, etc.	Your school will provide you with some examples and there may be some in your child's books/files. 1. Use coloured pencils or felts; 2. Choose a picture/word to go in the centre (the category name or topic title, e.g. rivers); 3. Draw four or five 'main roads' away from this central picture/word, each in a different colour; 4. Label these roads with the names and pictures of the main categories of the topic (e.g. water cycle, features, uses, settlements); 5. From each of these draw 'minor roads', again labelled with pictures/words to do with these sub-categories (e.g. power, leisure, transport, navigation). A mind map can be completed in one go or built up over a period of time. Let your child draw the images, use colour and print the words. There are computer programs available to construct mind maps – use Google to search for 'Tony Buzan'.	Mind maps are a great way to get lots of information down on paper quickly and in a fun way. They also help you to understand what you have written down and give you a useful way of revising for exams. Practise by making mind maps of your family tree, the different parts of your life, your favourite things on TV, etc.	

STRATEGY	PARENTS	STUDENT	COMMENTS Make notes to improve/adapt the strategy – discuss with the SENCO or TA
Word Books/Files These are personal banks of words arranged in categories (e.g. people, places, actions, feelings, etc.) rather than alphabetically. The category names and the number of categories used is flexible and depends on age and ability. This type of word book/dictionary helps students see how words are linked together by association. Each time it is used the student considers what the word means and is reminded of other words that are related to it, which are recorded in the same section. This strategy helps students to store words and remember them when they are needed.	Your child may bring a word book/file from school. If not, get him/her a small notebook file (A5 portrait is good). Ask the school for copies of category pictures. Choose about 15 categories, depending on your child's ability. You will need two sets. Discuss what each of the pictures represents. Stick one set on the inside cover and first page to form an index. The other set is divided throughout the book and placed one on the top right-hand corner of each category section. As your child asks for the spelling of the word, say 'What is it?'/'Where does it belong?' and help him/her to select the category from the index. The word is written on the page – adding a drawing can help with understanding and finding the word at another time. Arrange the words in alphabetical order on the category page if you wish.	Your own 'word book' or 'word file' helps you with understanding the meaning of words and with spelling. It is also useful if you can't think of the right word to use. Always have it with you and don't be afraid to ask adults to write words for you.	

Structure and Rules

Observed Behaviours

- Uses immature expressive language – missing words from sentences or confusing the word order.
- Speaks telegrammatically, i.e. using only the key words needed to convey a message.
- Struggles to understand complex grammatical structures such as connectives – 'and', 'so', 'but', 'to'.
- Makes grammatical errors in written work.
- Struggles to sequence ideas and thoughts and so has difficulty recalling events in the correct sequence or telling a story in the correct order.
- Has poor phonological awareness, i.e. sound knowledge of a word.
- Experiences difficulties learning new words, i.e. storing the sounds for a new word correctly, resulting in inaccurate use.

Positive Communication

1 Speak clearly – give clear, short instructions and chunk information. If you have an accent, be aware of regional terms you may use and how your phrasing may appear odd to your students. The larger the class, the slower you need to speak.

2 Keep sentences short and chunk information. Reduce the number of clauses and keep everything in the correct sequence, e.g. 'Genes are in chromosomes and chromosomes are in the nucleus of our cells' rather than 'The nucleus of all our cells contain chromosomes, where genes are found.'

3 Avoid correcting students' poor grammar; rather, use the correct form when replying, e.g. 'Her give me the wrong book, Miss', 'Oh, she gave you the wrong book, did she?'. When working on increasing the level of grammatical difficulty with the pupil, stress the key words but retain normal speech intonation.

4 Simplify words and sentences or repeat using a more simplified version, e.g. 'What are the comparisons and contrasts between Liverpool and London – what's the same and what's different about Liverpool and London?'

5   Be aware that the understanding of grammatical expression is closely linked to the ability to remember what has been said. Work on increasing the students' ability to understand using concrete objects. Make sure that they have a chance to familiarise themselves with the objects being used so that an immediate link is made with the object and the instruction.

Universal Strategies and Approaches

6   Work on tense in relation to time, using hand gestures. Place your left hand in front of you to indicate now/present; move it to your left-hand side to indicate before/past; move it to the right to indicate after/future, etc. Don't forget to reverse this if you are facing students.

7   Consider introducing class choral speaking/chanting to a range of subjects. Chanting mnemonics, dates linked to facts, information from science, etc., gives students the opportunity to practise the use of complex grammar and has the added benefit of supporting their ability to transfer facts into long-term memory.

8   Have a set of boxes available in the classroom labelled with basic elements of a sentence, such as people, actions, objects, places, adjectives. Collect pictures linked to topic work to go in each box. The student selects a picture from a selection of the boxes, e.g. a person, an action and an object then organise these pictures in sequence to make a sentence: 'The soldier is driving the tank.' Through questioning this can then be expanded to 'The young British soldier is driving the squad, in a tank, to the frontline.'

9   Improve narrative skills by working on shared stories/reports in small groups – the adult starts a story or a report about a visit/visitor, finishing in mid-sentence. Each student, in turn, continues the story/report, stopping when the adult raises their hand, until it is finished. As students become more confident, the activity could be recorded to support written work.

10 Use writing planners/frames across the curriculum – these are reminder cue cards/sheets that range from very simple to fairly complex. A simple version may include key question words (e.g. 'what?', 'where?', 'who?') together with a sequential set of questions linked to either a practical task (e.g. recording an investigation, writing up a field trip) or a piece of writing.

A more complex one would add questions/suggestions for each stage and a checklist at the end. A range of writing frames can be found in the *How to be Brilliant at . . .* series (see commercial resources).

11 Take a structured approach in developing narrative skills by teaching each element of narrative using a programme such as the Black Sheep Press resources and new ELCISS materials (see commercial resources).

12 Play 'snap' or 'pelmanism', matching formal/informal sentences, e.g. 'Hello Sally' versus 'Hi Sal'.

13 Use visual sentence planners to support grammatical understanding of modern foreign languages. Provide laminated strips divided into boxes and a write-on wipe-off pen. Discuss the structure of sentences and the differences with English, e.g.:

English			
Subject	Verb	Adjective	Object
I	*have*	*black*	*hair*

French			
Subject	Verb	Object	Adjective
J'	*ai*	*les cheveux*	*noirs*

Commercially Available Material

- Combimage – LDA
- BROGY – TaskMaster
- Grammar game boards – TaskMaster
- Silly Bulls – Philip & Tacey
- Communication in Print – Widgit Software
- Interactive Storytelling – Speechmark
- Narrative Intervention Programme – ELCISS
- KS2 Narrative – Black Sheep Press

Social Communication Skills

Observed Behaviours

- Lacks flexibility in use of language for a range of complex functions, e.g. to compliment others, express feelings, negotiate, suggest or reason.
- Experiences difficulties with conversational skills, including:
  - waiting for and taking a turn in a conversation
  - initiating and then maintaining a topic of conversation appropriately. A student may have a tendency to talk about a favourite topic.
  - repairing a breakdown when there is a misunderstanding
  - awareness of the listener's knowledge, providing either too much or too little information for the listener to understand.
- Finds it difficult to understand and use non-verbal communication skills, including eye contact, facial expressions, posture and proximity. A student may stand too close to others without realising the implications of this.
- Speaks too loudly for the situation.
- Takes the adult's role.
- Does not understand hidden meaning or intent, e.g. making a literal interpretation of what has been said. A lack of use of intent or implied meaning results in a student appearing overly honest or 'blunt'.
- Struggles to adapt and use language in a flexible way across different social situations.

Positive Communication

1 Do not assume anything. Constantly check understanding, especially in social situations.

2 Make rules explicit and model appropriate skills. Use peers as role models. Consistently identify what the student should do rather than should not do and record rules visually.

3 Signal changes in topic, e.g. 'We're now talking about the General Strike in 1926.'

4 During discussion time do not follow tangential replies. Re-direct the student back to the current topic of conversation, e.g. 'We're not talking about that now, we're talking about the miners' strike.'

5 Teach students how to cope during times such as 'changing for PE', using their lockers, arriving late for school, lost property, etc. Make sure they have guidelines for procedures and know where to go/who to ask if they forget.

6 Monitor students during group/sports activities to make sure they are on track. Brief them beforehand in ways that you may do this. Use symbol cue cards as discreet reminders, e.g. picture of a ball for 'focus on the ball', etc.

7 Question what happened when a student responds inappropriately to an instruction. Check that the instruction was not ambiguous or could be interpreted literally.

8 Students with severe social communication difficulties respond more readily if adults say 'The rule is…' rather than 'I want you to…' or 'You must…'

9 Distract and praise appropriate behaviour rather than draw attention to inappropriate behaviour.

10 Simplify language, particularly within cause-and-effect situations, e.g. 'You hurt Robert, he feels angry and upset.'

11 Use 'responsive listening' to help students when they are emotionally distressed. This strategy is a way of responding so that frustration is lowered rather than heightened. We all have difficulty expressing ourselves when emotions are running high, but for a student with SLCN this is a particularly difficult time. This is done by calmly 'echoing', in a neutral voice, what the distressed student's emotion appears to be rather than asking questions, giving advice or offering a solution. For example, 'You're very angry/upset', rather than 'Stop that, it isn't going to get you anywhere.'

12 Be careful when joking or using sarcasm – you may be taken literally. Make sure to explain what you mean when using ambiguous language. Use resources that interpret non-literal language, such as *White Elephants and Red Herrings* (see commercial resources).

13 Confirm that you have heard what he/she has said positively; 'Mmm' or a nod may not be understood.

Universal Strategies and Approaches

14 Develop students' ability to take responsibility for not understanding by creating a culture in the classroom that gives them the confidence to say if they (a) couldn't hear, (b) didn't understand the words you used or (c) had difficulty with the pace. Do this by specifically teaching them how to do it and praising them when they do. 'Seeking clarification' cue cards are useful for this.

15 Work on understanding the rules of sports and games. Ensure that students with poor memory and sequencing skills have the opportunity to learn rules thoroughly even if this has to be done one-to-one or in a small group.

16 Students with SLCN often struggle to tell and understand jokes. Provide opportunities for students to practise telling and or discussing jokes.

17 Spend time discussing situations: 'Why do we do this and not that?', 'Why is it sometimes okay not to tell the truth?', etc.

18 Help peers to understand that when a student with SLCN is 'reporting on others' or sticking to rules too rigorously, this is something he/she has difficulty with, and their support is needed to help him/her sort out what is socially acceptable and what is not.

19 Establish a home–school link book so that misunderstandings about lessons, homework, dates, school rules, peer relationships, etc., can be kept to a minimum. Make sure this book records only factual information. Do not use it to comment on the student's behaviour. Both home and school should record information to share.

20 Consider unstructured times (e.g. break-time, lunch-time, some open-ended classroom activities), as this can cause great anxiety and depends on the student's ability to make relationships and fill his/her time appropriately without direction. Some students with SLCN would benefit if they were involved in structured activities such as helping in the library, especially if they were getting some practice working as a team.

21 Provide the student with a regular, important job to do to help increase his/her feeling of worth. Choose one that is not open-ended nor relies on peer relationships to start with, gradually building in some interaction with others.

22 Always prepare students for possible changes in routine or personnel.

23 Use cue cards and posters with photographs, pictures or symbols to remind students of social communication skill rules, e.g. interrupting, taking turns, using eye contact.

Targeted Strategies and Approaches

24 Begin group work by identifying appropriate social communication skills for that specific activity. For instance, good listening, waiting for a turn to speak and looking at the speaker. Link this to social skills posters displayed around the school.

25 Support students in developing their emotional literacy by using the appropriate words when the emotion is being experienced. Picture cue cards are useful for this. Drama sessions offer an opportunity to role-play emotion and the class novel usually portrays characters' feelings, which can be linked to students' own experiences.

26 A fundamental social communication skill is to be able to take turns. Bring turn-taking into classroom activities. Use board games that are designed to reinforce/revise topic vocabulary so that it has a dual purpose.

27 Start your lesson with a short social skills ice-breaker.

28 Introduce 'talk time' – the opportunity for a student to talk to a 'listening buddy' about their favourite topics of conversation at a specified time during the day.

29 Introduce social stories (Smith 2003) to help children understand situations and how to respond and behave.

30 Set up a social communication skills group to focus on the development of specific social communication skills. Ensure students have opportunities to generalise skills in context by setting targets which can be supported in class and at home. Use commercially available programmes such as the *Talkabout. . .* series (see commercial resources below).

31 Use role-play to practise the use of communication skills in specific social situations – for instance, practising greetings, initiating conversations or giving a compliment.

32 Consider opportunities to develop social communication skills during break-times through 'buddy' systems.

33 Discuss how communication changes according to where you are/who you are talking to. Practise, through role-play, the different language styles/ behaviour required for a range of settings, e.g. church, library, restaurant, supermarket, etc.

34 Practise simple sentences with different voices and emphasis.

35 Develop the use of mime and gesture in small groups.

Commercially Available Material

- 'Group rules' poster – Language for Learning
- 'Active listening' cue cards – Language for Learning
- 'Seeking clarification' cue cards – Language for Learning
- Talkabout – Speechmark
- Talkabout activities – Speechmark
- Talkabout DVD – Speechmark
- Talkabout Relationships – Speechmark

- Talkabout for Teenagers – Speechmark
- Talking About Conversation – Blacksheep Press
- Quality Circle Time in the Secondary School – David Fulton Publishers
- Contact I: A Structured Approach to Teaching Non-verbal Behaviours – Surer Steps
- Emotions photo cards – LDA
- Don't Take it So Literally – Winslow
- What Did You Say? What Did You Mean? – Jessica Kingsley
- Mystifying Metaphors and Smiley Similes – BirdArt
- Red Herrings & White Elephants – Metro Publishing
- 'Good listening, talking & waiting' posters – TaskMaster
- An Asperger Dictionary of Everyday Expressions – Jessica Kingsley
- 'Social behaviour' colour cards – Speechmark
- Feeling Up or Feeling Down? – Speechmark
- Bullying Ups and Downs? – Speechmark
- Teaching Happiness – Speechmark
- Writing & Developing Social Stories – Speechmark
- The Social Skills Handbook – Speechmark
- Practical Ways to Support Pupils with Autism Spectrum Disorders in the Secondary School – Winslow
- Teen Issues – Speechmark
- What Are They Thinking? – Speechmark

Using Strategies at Home

STRATEGY	PARENTS	STUDENT	COMMENTS Make notes to improve/adapt the strategy – discuss with the SENCO or TA
Social Skills Prompting There are a number of skills used in social situations that help with communication and developing good relationships with other people. Some students find these skills very difficult to learn. Social communication skills groups are often set up in schools to systematically teach students these skills. Students need to practise regularly and in as many different situations as possible.	The SENCO in your school will tell you what is being taught in your child's social skills group. Use the same picture/symbol cards and words that are being used in school. Discuss the situation that your child is going into, reminding him/her of what he/she should say/do. Remember that the rule should be for life, so teach what is acceptable in most situations (e.g. say 'excuse me' rather than tap someone on the shoulder, etc.)	Practise what you have been doing in your social skills group at school. Let your family help by working out some 'secret codes'. Discuss how you did afterwards. Ask your parents which of their/your friends and family are good people to copy.	

Memory Skills

Observed Behaviours

- Forgets instructions easily.

- Does not record homework accurately (given verbally).

- Struggles to follow long and complex instructions despite appearing to listen.

- Forgets stages within an activity.

- Forgets equipment.

- Responds to just the beginning or the end of an instruction.

- Has difficulty following instructions; the student may be unable to repeat or recall what needs to be done in the correct order.

- Gets lost within an activity or when giving information.

- Loses track in a conversation or a discussion. The student may appear to repeat themselves frequently.

- Needs more time to process language.

- Jumps to the wrong conclusions or gives a tangential reply based on only part of the information given.

- Becomes easily confused, particularly during fast conversations or discussions.

- Lacks organisational skills.

Positive Communication

1 Simplify language, speak slowly and introduce new words gradually.

2 Avoid or explain non-literal language.

3 Use gesture/mime to support verbal language.

4 Understanding is closely linked to the ability to remember. Give students time to process what has been said by using the ten-second rule – once you have given an instruction allow up to ten seconds for a response. During this time, consider the instruction: were there too many words? Was the vocabulary too difficult to understand? If the student does not respond after ten seconds, either rephrase the instruction or, if the right level of language was used the first time, simply repeat the instruction.

Universal Strategies and Approaches

5 We tend to remember best what we learn at the beginning and end of a lesson. Maximise on this by creating breaks which provide several beginnings and several endings. Repeat the main teaching points at these times.

6 Build in revising and recalling with fun activities such as word definition games, word searches and group cartoon drawings related to the topic.

7 Support pupils by teaching techniques that aid memory and encourage them to take responsibility for using external memories such as lists, drawing key points, learning mnemonics, drawing mind maps, etc.

8 Encourage students to 'rehearse' what they have heard by saying it over and over silently. (This may have to be done out loud to begin with.)

9 Give instructions in the same order as the action required, e.g. 'Finish the sentence you are writing, then get your homework books', rather than 'Get your homework books after you have finished the sentence you are writing.'

10 Practise remembering the key points by counting on fingers, rehearsing and visualising what has to be done.

11 Use mind maps as these present a wealth of information in a memorable format, particularly if students are visual learners. Provide wall-size mind maps of the current class topic to act as a reminder of key points studied so far.

12 Use mnemonics for anything that is sequenced or contains a set number of features, e.g. MRS NERG for the seven life processes: movement, reproduction, sensitivity, nutrition, excretion, respiration and growth.

13 For instant recall (word finding) help students to store words efficiently by working on word association. The 'understanding the meaning of words' strategy section has a range of word definition/sorting and classifying activities.

14 Support students' ability to remember instructions by using task-management boards which provide pictorial and/or written support of the stages within a single activity.

15 Provide visual timetables that incorporate what has to be remembered at home, such as homework, swimming things, library books, etc.

16 Train students to say key points out loud, then whisper them, then 'think' them.

17 Encourage note-taking both when listening to information (hold up a notebook as you repeat every key word so students know what to record) and during discussion times so that students remember the points they want to make.

Targeted Strategies and Approaches

18 Give students a verbal message to give to another member of staff or class. The message should require an answer so that it is clear that the instruction was delivered correctly and the reply remembered.

19 Arrange pictures representing key components of current topic work on the table. Objects are removed while students look away; they then have to guess what is missing.

20 Play versions of 'I went to market and I bought...' using current topic vocabulary. For example, the first student might say: 'I'm going to make a tie-dyed scarf so I will need some cotton material.' The second student responds, 'I'm going to make a tie-dyed scarf so I will need some cotton material and some bees' wax.' To extend demands on memory, add more elements to the sentence.

21 Provide opportunities for students to practise sequences so that memory is improved. For example, in line dancing, rehearsal increases the ability to remember longer dance sequences.

22 Provide prompt cards with (a) basic facts such as address, date of birth, days of the week, numbers and spellings of numbers, months of the year, tables, etc., and (b) main points of discussion.

23 Link new information to raps, jingles and songs to maximise the ability to remember.

24 Teach visualisation skills. Ask students to imagine something they do everyday, e.g. going through their front door, walking into the hall and up the stairs then into their bedroom. Ask them to think about the pictures they 'see'. Practise doing this with information – for example, can they 'see' people queuing for food with their ration books? Ask them to describe what clothes people are wearing, what sort of shop it is, what the weather is like, etc.

Commercially Available Material

- Kidspiration and Inspiration – Semerc
- Mind Maps for Kids – Thorsons
- Mind Maps for Kids: Rev up for Revision – Thorsons
- The Mind Map Book: Radiant Thinking – BBC Books

Speech

> **Observed Behaviours**
>
> - Says multi-syllabic or complex words inaccurately.
> - Simplifies words.
> - Experiences difficulties with intelligibility within connected speech.
> - Is dysfluent, i.e. may stammer.

It is difficult to offer activities that benefit students in school who have specific speech problems. Seek advice from the local speech and language therapy service about the difficulties experienced by individual students and their needs in school.

1 Try not to single out students with articulation problems to practise sounds. This is unhelpful and can hinder progress. 'Sound' work is better done in small groups with advice from your speech and language therapy service.

2 Deal with teasing from classmates positively, so that pupils' self-esteem does not suffer.

Positive Communication

3 Do not pretend to understand a student if he/she is unintelligible. They usually know, and this makes them feel that what they have to say is not important. Rather, ask for a repetition using different words; this way the student knows he/she is worth communicating with.

4 Confirm that you have understood what has been said by repeating some of the information – for example, 'So you are going to the dentist on Tuesday', etc. This relaxes the pupil and gives him/her the confidence to continue.

5 Make sure that the student in question can see how you speak. Face-to-face, speak slowly and clearly.

6 Try not to ask the student to repeat sounds back to you 'correctly'. This will have little long-term effect. For example, if as an adult you were asked to repeat the word 'loch' with a Scottish accent, you would have little difficulty; however, if asked to pronounce the same 'ch' sound in other words every time the 'ck' sound occurred, it would be very difficult.

Targeted Strategies and Approaches

7 Where possible, liaise with the speech and language therapist if a student in your class accesses speech and language therapy. There will be a programme of work that can be supported and reinforced in school.

8 For those students with severe speech difficulties, use visual support to ensure that they can be effective when communicating. A simple communication board with key vocabulary (pictures and words) for specific times of the day can be used so the student can point to the pictures while talking.

Thinking Skills

Observed Behaviours

- Experiences difficulties using language for complex functions, e.g. to reason, evaluate, plan, negotiate, engage in debate.
- Struggles to assimilate all of the necessary information, leading to misunderstandings.
- Fails to consider the viewpoint of others.
- Lacks organisational skills.

Positive Communication

1 Keep sentences short and chunk information. Reduce the number of clauses and keep everything in the correct sequence, e.g. 'Genes are in chromosomes and chromosomes are in the nucleus of our cells', rather than 'The nucleus of all our cells contain chromosomes, where genes are found.'

2 Simplify words and sentences or repeat using a more simple version, e.g. 'What hypotheses can we raise from looking at this tapestry?', 'What does this tapestry suggest to you – what does it make you think about?'

3 Develop your questioning skills so that you encourage thinking. Grade your use of questions words from easy to hard: 'who', 'what', 'when', 'where' before 'how' and 'why'. Use symbol cue cards representing each one for students who find them confusing.

4 Teach the meaning of the terminology used to direct students' work, e.g. compare/contrast, illustrate, consider, predict, evaluate, etc. Simple activities such as 'pairs' can make this palatable. Pair the terminology with a simpler version, e.g. 'create' and 'make'. Students sort them into pairs. A useful tool to support vocabulary teaching is *Bringing Words to Life* (see commercial resources).

Universal Strategies and Approaches

5   When introducing a new topic, start with objects and pictures. Use this visual material to encourage students to think about and discuss the information they can find in them. Introduce the new, specific vocabulary to this discussion so that students begin to use it as soon as possible. Support this stage by providing vocabulary cards with the word, picture and a short definition. Encourage questioning by providing question cards to cue students in. When students can discuss the topic well, are familiar with the concepts/theories and can ask and answer questions appropriately, introduce note-taking. This can be done in a number of ways, depending on the students' preferred learning styles.

6   Provide worksheets with note-taking boxes. Each box represents an area within the topic and contains questions prompting the student to record relevant information. Students can draw pictures or write single words/ short sentences.

7   Provide recording forms divided into key elements for analysis.

8   Mind maps, developed by Tony Buzan, see p. 141, support thinking skills in a number of ways – a range of information can be considered at one time, connections between information/ideas/concepts are made and linked to the appropriate words.

9   Provide colour-coded text to accompany any worksheet that requires the student to read, process information and answer questions in his/her own words. Simply highlight the question and the part of the text that contains the answer to that question with the same colour highlighter pen.

10   Give out written summaries of lessons. This will help students to retain the main points and gives them a framework for follow-up work. It gives the SLCN student the confidence to 'stick with the lesson' even if they don't fully understand or their concentration has waned.

11   Provide a range of sorting and classifying exercises, encouraging students to sort information in a number of ways to support a higher level of understanding.

12 Work on recording information visually, e.g. Venn diagrams, flow charts, prioritisation pyramids, tables (pros and cons), etc. Start by using diagrams to support information gathering. (Link this to strategy 3 above.)

13 Spend time working on 'cause and effect' and 'prediction'. Start with personal experiences before moving on to current topic work. Again, provide writing spaces to help students organise information.

14 Play DVDs/present information back-to-back – use the first time for asking students to look out for key areas and the second time for note-taking. Utilise mind mapping. Give students a mind map with the main roads (key areas) marked. They then add the minor roads and key words during the second playing/presentation.

15 Make a 'thinking skills' poster for the classroom wall as a checklist for students when they are working on assignments. Discuss the skills and provide suitable recording frames for each skill. Include: planning, ordering, sorting, solving problems, creating ideas, deciding, choosing, classifying, comparing and predicting.

16 Consider using the following resources: 'Six thinking hats', 'Top ten thinking tactics', 'Mind manager', 'Mind genius', 'Inspiration' – see details in *A Thinking Classroom*, listed below.

17 Teach visualisation skills. Ask students to imagine something they do everyday, e.g. going through their front door, walking into the hall and up the stairs then into their bedroom. Ask them to think about the pictures they 'see'. Practise doing this with information – for example, can they 'see' people queuing for food with their ration books? Ask them to describe what clothes people are wearing, what sort of shop it is, what the weather is like, etc.

Commercially Available Resources

- Study Strategies Made Easy – Winslow
- How to be Brilliant at ... Recording series – Brilliant Publications
- A Thinking Classroom (primary, but great ideas) – LDA
- Accelerated Learning in the Classroom – Network Educational Press
- Transforming Thinking Philosophical Inquiry in the Primary and Secondary Classroom – Routledge

Glossary

Terminology and jargon can be confusing and can easily lead to a breakdown in communication amongst professionals and parents. This glossary lists a range of terms linked to language skills, SLCN and school-based support that may be found within specialist reports.

Articulation	Control of speech organs in order to produce speech sounds.
Articulatory/ Verbal Dyspraxia	A motor-programming disorder, which involves difficulties in programming the sequence of movements required to produce continuous speech.
Asperger's Syndrome	An autism spectrum condition first described by Hans Asperger, characterised by social interaction difficulties, all-absorbing narrow interests, the need for routine and motor clumsiness.
Attention control	The ability to maintain focus.
Attention deficit (hyperactivity) disorder	A disorder affecting attention control where the young person is easily distracted. Hyperactivity is where the young person shows high levels of restlessness as well.
Auditory discrimination	The ability to hear the difference in sounds.
Auditory memory	The ability to remember information that is heard.
Autism spectrum disorder (ASD)	Young people with an autism spectrum condition experience impairments of social interaction, social communication and flexibility of thought. An autism spectrum condition is a lifelong developmental disability.
Cleft lip	A split in the upper lip, which occurs during foetal development, usually associated with cleft palate.
Cleft palate	A structural abnormality whereby the roof of the mouth is not formed properly, causing problems with eating, breathing, articulation and hearing. Often occurs with a cleft lip.

Conductive hearing loss	A hearing impairment caused by a difficulty in transmitting sound through the outer or middle ear.
Delayed language development	Language development follows the normal sequence and pattern but at a slower rate.
Disordered language development	Language development does not follow the normal pattern, giving rise to complex language problems in one or more specific areas of language.
Dysarthria	A difficulty caused by damage to the central nervous system (neurological), which results in loss of muscle control for speech.
Dysfluency	A difficulty in producing smooth, fluent speech. This term includes stammering (UK)/stuttering (USA).
Echolalia	The repetition of words or phrases heard without understanding. Echolalia can be delayed or immediate.
Expressive language	The use of words and sentences to convey a message.
Fluctuating hearing loss	Caused when children suffer from repeated colds or catarrhal infections, often undetected as the child is 'clear' at the time of hearing check, but can have a significant effect on language development.
Global development delay	The young person experiences a delay in all areas of development.
Inclusion Development Programme (IDP)	Part of the government's strategy to support children and young people with SEN. Provides support for leadership teams in schools and settings and professional development materials for school staff. Eight units for SLCN are available online.
Intonation	The rising and falling pitch patterns of language that express a wide range of meaning.
Language Master	A simple portable audio/visual device using cards striped with magnetic tape to provide auditory and visual information simultaneously.
Mnemonic	An aid to memory, e.g. initial letters of a sentence to spell a word or a picture accompanying a word.

Morphology	The way in which word structures change to signal a change in meaning, e.g. sleep, sleeping, slept, asleep.
Otitis media	The most common form of conductive hearing loss, caused by catarrhal infections spreading to the middle ear via the Eustachian tube.
Phoneme	The individual sounds we use when pronouncing sounds. There are approximately 40 in the English language.
Phonological awareness	The ability to think consciously about speech sounds and to use these skills within literacy.
Phonological delay	Phonological development follows a typical pattern, but at a slower rate. Phonological processes appear to persist beyond the age at which they should disappear, e.g. reduction of clusters, so *sl* in **sl***eeping* becomes *seeping*.
Phonological disorder	Phonological development does not follow a typical pattern of development, i.e. phonological processes which do not occur during typical development are present.
Phonology	The *speech* sound system of a language – the rules which govern how sounds are organised in words in order to convey different meanings.
Pragmatics	The use of language in social situations, including conversational skills and the understanding and use of non-verbal communication.
Receptive language	Understanding spoken language.
Selective mutism	A young person does not speak in certain situations, e.g. school, but can speak in others, e.g. home.
Semantics	The meaning of words and sentences.
Sensori-neural hearing loss	Severe deafness as a result of damage to the inner ear or nerve pathways to the brain.
Signalong	A system of hand shapes and movements which relate to the spoken grammatical form of English and can therefore be used to illustrate what the speaker is saying.
Social communication skills	*See* pragmatics.

Specific language impairment (SLI)	A primary, specific, persistent receptive or expressive language disorder/impairment in the absence of any other difficulties. It does not include children or young people who do not develop language because of intellectual or physical disability, hearing loss, emotional problems or environmental deprivation.
Speech, language and communication framework (SLCF)	Recognised competency framework published by The Communication Trust, setting out the knowledge and skills required by those working with children and young people with SLCN.
Speech, language and communication needs (SLCN)	A wide-ranging term used to encompass all speech, language and communication difficulties, e.g. difficulties communicating effectively with others; understanding and/or using language. Includes a range of complexity of needs from long-term persistent communication disabilities through to more transient language delay as a result of limited life experiences.
Stammering (stuttering)	*See* dysfluency.
Syntax	The rule system which governs the structure of language at a word, phrase and sentence level.
Theory of mind	Awareness that others have different thoughts, feelings and knowledge from yourself.

Bibliography

AFASIC (2010) *Transfer to Secondary School*. London: AFASIC.

Ayre, A. and Roulstone, S. (2009) *Transition to Secondary School: Supporting Pupils with Speech, Language and Communication Needs – Report to The Communication Trust*. London: The Communication Trust.

Buzan, T. (2003) *Mind Maps for Kids*. London: Thorsons.

Clegg, J., Stackhouse, J., Finch, K., Murphy, C. and Nicholls, S. (2009) 'Language abilities of secondary age pupils at risk of school exclusion: a preliminary report', *Child Language Teaching and Therapy*, Vol. 25, No. 1, pp. 123–129.

DCSF (2008) *The Bercow Report: A Review of Services for Children and Young People (0–19) With Speech, Language and Communication Needs*. Nottingham: DCSF.

DCSF (2010) *Coaching Your Teenager*. Nottingham: DCSF.

DCSF (2011) *Inclusion Development Plan*. Nottingham: DCSF.

DfES (2003) *Every Child Matters*. London: The Stationery Office.

Hayden, S. and Jordan, E. (2007) *Language for Learning: A Practical Guide for Supporting Pupils with Language and Communication Difficulties Across the Curriculum*. Oxon: Routledge.

ICAN (2006) *The Cost to the Nation of Children's Poor Communication*. London: ICAN.

Joffe, V. (2009) *What Teachers Want and Need to Know about Enhancing Speech, Language and Communication in the Classroom*. Presentation given to The Communication Trust Conference, London.

Joffe, V. (2011) 'Secondary school is not too late to support and enhance language and communication (ELCISS)', *AFASIC*, Winter, pp. 11–13.

Johnson, M. and Player, C. (2009) *Active Listening for Active Learning*. Stafford: QED Publications.

Lindsay, G., Dockrell, J., Desforges, M., Law, J. and Peacey, N. (2010) 'Meeting the needs of children and young people with speech, language and communication difficulties', *International Journal of Language and Communication Disorders*, Vol. 45, No. 4, pp. 448–460.

Myers, L. and Botting, N. (2008) 'Literacy in the mainstream inner-city school: its relationship to spoken language', *Child Language Teaching and Therapy*, Vol. 24, No. 1, pp. 95–114.

Ripley, K. and Barrett, J. (2008) *Supporting Speech, Language and Communication Needs*. London: Sage Publications.

Smith, C. (2003) *Writing & Developing Social Stories*. Oxford: Speechmark.

Speake, J. (2003) *How to Identify and Support Children with Speech and Language Difficulties*. Wisbech: LDA.

Spencer, S. (2007) *Language and Social Disadvantage: Does Language Play a Role in the Attainment and Outcomes of Mainstream Secondary Age Pupils in Areas of Social Disadvantage?* Presentation at AFASIC Fourth International Symposium.

Spencer, S., Clegg, J., Stackhouse, J. and Leicester, S. (2006) *Language and Social Disadvantage: A Preliminary Study of the Impact of Social Disadvantage at Secondary School Age*, Proceedings of the Royal College of Speech and Language Therapists Conference, May.

Stringer, H. (2006) *Effective Intervention with Secondary School Students with Speech and Language Disorder and Behaviour Problems: A Pilot Study*. Proceedings of NAPLIC Day Conference, March.

The Communication Trust (2008) *The Speech, Language and Communication Framework (SLCF)*.

The Communication Trust (2009) *Sentence Trouble*. London: The Communication Trust.

The Communication Trust (2009b) *Transition to Secondary School*. London: The Communication Trust.

The Communication Trust (2010a) *Speech, Language and Communication Information for Secondary Schools*. London: The Communication Trust.

The Communication Trust (2010b) *Don't Get Me Wrong: Information for Supporting Children and Young People with Speech, Language and Communication Needs*. London: The Communication Trust.

Wilson, G., Nash, M. and Earl, G. (2010) 'Supporting students with language learning difficulties in secondary schools through collaboration: the use of concept maps to investigate the impact on teachers' knowledge of vocabulary teaching', *Child Language Teaching and Therapy*, Vol. 26, No. 2, pp. 163–179.

Websites

Talking Point: www.talkingpoint.org.uk
AFASIC: www.afasic.org.uk
NASEN: www.nasen.org.uk
The Communication Trust: www.thecommunicationtrust.org.uk
NAPLIC: www.naplic.org.uk

Appendix: Suppliers of the Commercially Available Material

Supplier	Website
BBC Books	www.bbcshop.com
BirdArt	www.speelang.co.uk
Black Sheep Press	www.blacksheeppress.co.uk
Brilliant Publications	www.brilliantpublications.co.uk
CGP	www.cgpbooks.co.uk
Collins	www.collinseducation.com
ELCISS	www.elciss.com
Guilford Press	www.guilford.com
Jessica Kingsley	www.jkp.com
Language for Learning	www.languageforlearning.co.uk
LDA	www.ldalearning.com
Letts Education	www.lettsandlonsdale.com
Philip & Tacey Ltd	www.philipandtacey.co.uk
QED	www.qed.uk.com
Questions Publications	www.questionsonlinecatalogue.co.uk
Routledge	www.routledge.co.uk
Semerc	www.semerc.com
Smartkids	www.smartkids.co.uk
Speechmark	www.speechmark.net
Surer Steps	www.surersteps.co.uk
Taskmaster	www.taskmasteronline.co.uk
Thorsons	www.harpercollins.co.uk
Widgit Software Ltd	www.widgit.com
Winslow	www.winslow-cat.com
Yellow Door	www.yellow-door.net

Language for Learning in the Secondary School Training

Language for Learning offers training courses for school staff

Informative, practical and realistic

These ideas can be easily transferred into the classroom. The course has given me ideas to use with the whole class

Half & Whole day Training courses

Practical Workshops

Beautifully created and presented

Identification & assessment	Providing visual support
Improving social communication skills	Developing memory / Developing listening skills
Supporting vocabulary development	Providing access across the curriculum

Developed in 2000 by Sue Hayden and Emma Jordan, Language for Learning is a joint health and education non-profit making project owned by Worcestershire County Council and Worcestershire PCT. It provides training courses and resources for practitioners and parents from early years to key stage 4 and training materials for trainers to deliver these courses within their own authorities.

Language for Learning, Speech & Language Centre,
Franche Clinic, Marlpool Place, Kidderminster,
Worcestershire, DY11 5BB
Tel: 01562 751866

www.languageforlearning.co.uk

Language *for* Learning

supporting pupils with communication difficulties

Index

Glossary entries are in *italic*.

T - #0053 - 270723 - C160 - 297/210/9 - PB - 9780415619752 - Gloss Lamination